ROOTED IN CULTURE

BUILDING LIFE LESSONS TO NAVIGATE LIFE'S CHALLENGES

Robert Pene

Copyright © 2022 Robert Pene

All rights reserved.

ISBN: 9798370226373

DEDICATION

This book is dedicated to my Pene family from Faga'alu and my Passi family from Fagatogo. To all my cousins who we shared great memories of playing Nintendo, sports, running up and down the streets and climbing to the waterfalls, I'm grateful for all of you. And especially to my parents, aunts, uncles, and grandparents...I'm deeply indebted to your leadership and grace.

ACKNOWLEDGMENTS

I would like to acknowledge God and his grace for allowing me the motivation to do what I do with the talents He's blessed me with.

CONTENTS

INTRODUCTION 6

HI, I'M ROB PENE 13

FROM AMERICAN SAMOA 20

TONY SOLAITA LITTLE LEAGUE 26

IMPORTANCE OF CULTURAL HERITAGE 33

EXTRACTING LIFE PRINCIPLES 39

BE A STUDENT OF YOURSELF 48

INTERVIEW OTHERS ABOUT YOU 56

ORGANIZE THE DATA 66

CRAFT YOUR MANIFESTO 74

OVERCOMING SETBACKS 84

COMMIT TO MEMORY AND PRACTICE 94

BUILDING A SUPPORT SYSTEM 104

APPLYING PRINCIPLES IN DIFFERENT LIFE CONTEXTS 115

NORMALIZE THE MISSION 129

DEVELOPING A PERSONAL GROWTH PLAN 139

REVISIT AND EVOLVE YOUR PRINCIPLES OVER TIME 147

CONCLUSION 159

SPECIAL BONUS SECTIONS 165

REFLECTIVE PRAYERS 205

REFLECTIVE PRAYERS FOR EACH CHAPTER 209

ABOUT THE AUTHOR 226

INTRODUCTION

"Life isn't about finding yourself. Life is about creating yourself." — George Bernard Shaw

Life is full of unexpected turns, challenges, and moments that test our character. In these moments, we must anchor ourselves to something deeper—our principles.

But what if those principles were not just abstract concepts, but powerful, living guides shaped by our unique stories, experiences, and cultural heritage?

Imagine a tree deeply rooted in fertile soil. No matter how fierce the storm, it bends but does not break. Like that tree, we too must root ourselves deeply—in our values, in our experiences, and in the cultures that shape us. This book is about defining those roots and using them to navigate life with clarity and resilience.

My story begins on a small, lush island in the Pacific—American Samoa—where the green mountains meet the blue waters, and the warmth of a tight-knit community is felt everywhere. Growing up, I was surrounded by strong values of family, respect, humility, and community.

These principles weren't just taught; they were lived every day. Whether it was gathering for Sunday meals, playing sports with friends, or listening to the wisdom of my elders, these experiences became the bedrock of my identity.

But as much as I loved my island home, I knew there was more for me to explore—more dreams to chase. Driven by this determination, I earned a full baseball and academic scholarship to Spring Arbor University in Michigan, where I played under the legendary coach, Hank Burbridge.

My journey took me from the intimate fields of American Samoa to the college baseball diamonds of the U.S., and later to coaching fields across Europe. Each step challenged me to grow, adapt, and draw strength from my cultural roots.

From these early days, my Polynesian heritage has been a constant source of strength. It has shaped my values, informed my decisions, and guided me through both triumphs and challenges. Whether working with high-profile business owners, athletes, or coaches, or serving as a roadshow coach for Major League Baseball in Europe, I've always leaned on the lessons of my culture. It was in these moments, far from home, that I learned to appreciate my own heritage even more. I understood that our values and norms deeply influence who we are and how we navigate life.

There were many times when I had to turn inward, relying on my heritage to remind me of my uniqueness and what I bring to the world. Often, we overlook the details that make us who we are, which can be detrimental to our growth. But when you understand yourself—truly know who you are—the possibilities are endless.

This book is a guide to help you define your own principles, draw from the richness of your own heritage, and build a life that is authentically yours. It is about becoming a lifelong student of yourself, embracing setbacks as stepping stones, and finding strength in your unique story. Together, we will explore how to live by your principles in every aspect of life—from relationships to leadership, from personal growth to community engagement.

You don't need to have it all figured out; none of us do. But by grounding yourself in who you truly are and where you come from, you can navigate life's challenges with resilience and purpose. As you turn these pages, I invite you to embark on a journey of self-discovery, reflection, and growth. Let's dig deep, find our roots, and grow stronger together.

What You'll Discover in This Book:

- **Defining Your Core Principles:** How to identify and articulate the values that matter most to you.

- **Drawing from Your Heritage:** Using your cultural background and personal stories as a source of strength and wisdom.

- **Overcoming Setbacks with Resilience:** How to adapt without losing your essence and turn challenges into opportunities.

- **Applying Principles Across Life Contexts:** Practical strategies to live authentically in relationships, career, community, and more.

- **Creating a Living Manifesto:** A step-by-step guide to crafting a personal manifesto that evolves with you.

This is not just a book—it's a blueprint for living with intention, authenticity, and strength. Are you ready to dig deeper?

Welcome to "Rooted in Culture: Building Life Lessons to Navigate Life's Challenges." I'm Rob Pene, a marketing entrepreneur, proud Polynesian, former professional baseball player, and a lifelong learner committed to growth and self-discovery.

My hope for you, as you read this book, is that you will gain insight into a systematic process for uncovering and unpacking your own story. I want you to experience intentional growth, be empowered to live authentically, and, most importantly, help others find their purpose too.

Thank you for being here. Let's embark on this journey together.

QUOTABLES FROM THIS SECTION

> *"Our roots are the anchors that hold us steady through life's storms."*

> *"To live with purpose, we must first understand the principles that guide us."*

> *"Your story is your power; use it to create the life you want."*

DISCUSSION QUESTIONS

1. What does it mean to be "rooted in culture"? How do your cultural roots shape who you are today?

2. Reflect on a time when your values were tested. How did you respond, and what did you learn?

3. How can understanding your story and heritage serve as a guide for navigating life's challenges?

HI, I'M ROB PENE

"The journey of a thousand miles begins with one step." — *Lao Tzu*

Hi, I'm Rob Pene—a marketing entrepreneur, proud Polynesian, former professional baseball player, and a lifelong learner committed to growth and self-discovery.

My story is shaped by the vibrant landscapes of American Samoa and the values deeply rooted in my culture. But beyond the places I've been and the titles I've held, my journey has been about one thing: understanding what it means to live authentically and with purpose.

I was raised in two small villages, Faga'alu and Fagatogo, where family wasn't just the people you lived with—it was the heartbeat of the community.

My days were spent in the embrace of my mother, Cita, and my father, High Chief Gaisoa Savalivali Seigafolava Ropati Pene, along with my sister, Betty, and countless cousins, aunts, uncles, and grandparents.

It was here that I learned the meaning of togetherness—not just through shared meals or games, but through the silent lessons of everyday life: the way my parents navigated challenges, showed respect to others, and worked tirelessly to provide for us.

A Lesson in Resilience and Adaptability: While my upbringing in Samoa taught me the power of cultural heritage, it was my journey beyond the island that taught me the art of adaptation. I left home with a dream and a scholarship in hand, moving from the familiar mountains and waters of Samoa to the foreign fields of Michigan.

Playing under Coach Hank Burbridge was a masterclass in perseverance and humility. There were days when everything seemed foreign and difficult—when I felt the sting of being different, the isolation of being far from home. But these moments pushed me to rely on my roots and taught me that growth happens when we lean into discomfort, not away from it.

Finding Strength in Cultural Bridges: As I moved further into the world, from business meetings with high-profile clients to coaching young athletes in Europe, I realized that the core of who we are doesn't have to change to fit in; rather, it can serve as a bridge to understanding and connecting with others.

My heritage became my lens to see the world and a toolkit to navigate it. I learned to see my culture not as something that set me apart, but as something that enriched every experience, every conversation, and every challenge.

Building Systems for Intentional Living: Reflecting on my journey, I've realized that the true essence of my growth lies in intentionality. I've come to understand that our lives are shaped not just by what happens to us, but by how we choose to respond.

Growing up in a close-knit community taught me to value relationships, but it also taught me to be discerning about the connections I keep. Today, I often ask myself:

- Is this relationship nourishing, or does it feel forced?

- Are the people around me aligned with values of kindness, support, and truthfulness?

- Do we create spaces where we feel safe, seen, and heard?

These reflections guide me in both my personal life and my business endeavors. I believe in creating systems that allow for growth, both for myself and for those around me. This means continually reassessing my goals, staying true to my principles, and being willing to adapt without losing sight of who I am.

A Call to Look Inward: In "Rooted in Culture: Building Life Lessons to Navigate Life's Challenges," I aim to share not just my story, but the frameworks and processes that have helped me live with intention.

My hope is that you, too, can draw from your unique experiences, heritage, and values to craft a life that feels true to you. The lessons we learn from our past and our culture are not meant to be kept; they are meant to be shared, lived, and expanded upon.

As you read this book, I encourage you to look inward, reflect on your own journey, and find the principles that will guide you. Our stories may start in different places, but the quest for authenticity, growth, and purpose is a universal one. Let's embark on this path together and uncover the lessons that lie within each of us.

Quotables from this section

> *"Understanding what it means to live authentically starts with embracing who you are."*

> *"Growth happens when we lean into discomfort, not away from it."*

> *"Your heritage is not a barrier but a bridge to connect and thrive."*

Discussion Questions

1. How does Rob's story of navigating different environments and cultures resonate with your own experiences?

   _____
   _____
   _____

2. What does living authentically mean to you? How can you practice authenticity in your daily life?

   _____
   _____
   _____

3. Discuss a time when discomfort led to personal growth. What did that experience teach you?

   _____
   _____
   _____

FROM AMERICAN SAMOA

"A people without the knowledge of their past history, origin, and culture is like a tree without roots." — Marcus Garvey

American Samoa, a small island nation nestled in the South Pacific Ocean, is made up of five rugged islands and two coral atolls.

As the easternmost territory of the United States, it remains a unique blend of Polynesian and Western influences, where time seems to slow down and community takes center stage.

Growing up here meant being part of a vibrant culture deeply rooted in traditions, respect, and family values—principles that shape every aspect of daily life.

From a young age, I was immersed in the traditions and customs of the Samoan people, whose ancestors have lived on these islands for thousands of years. Samoan society is organized around the 'aiga (extended family), and life in our villages revolves around communal responsibilities and shared experiences.

This closeness creates a bond that is hard to describe—a sense of belonging that goes beyond bloodlines, connecting us to each other and to the land we call home.

Our culture places a strong emphasis on respect—for elders, for authority, and for the natural environment. We learned early on that every action has meaning, every word carries weight, and every person plays a role in the greater fabric of the community.

The concept of "fa'a Samoa," or the Samoan way, is not just a set of rules but a living, breathing philosophy. It teaches us to honor our ancestors, take pride in our heritage, and navigate life with humility, grace, and a spirit of service.

Spirituality is woven into the very fabric of our culture. Though most Samoans today are devout Christians, there is a deep-rooted respect for the old ways, where traditional Polynesian beliefs and the worship of ancestral spirits still linger in the stories passed down through generations.

These spiritual traditions remind us that we are merely stewards of the land and the sea, bound to respect and protect them for those who come after us.

But it's not just the rich cultural tapestry that makes American Samoa special—it's the breathtaking natural beauty that surrounds us. Imagine a place where emerald mountains rise up from the ocean, their peaks often shrouded in mist, and where the turquoise waters lap gently against white sandy shores.

The islands are a sanctuary of lush rainforests teeming with life, cascading waterfalls that provide a backdrop to our daily lives, and coral reefs that serve as both food source and protector. This is the land that nurtures us, and in turn, we nurture it.

Life on the island is simple yet profound. Days are marked by the rhythm of the ocean, the crowing of roosters at dawn, and the gathering of family at dusk.

There is a saying in Samoan: "E leai se mea e sili atu i le alofa," which means "There is nothing greater than love." This love is not just for family but for our culture, our land, and our community. It is this love that binds us together, guiding us through life's challenges and celebrating life's joys.

American Samoa is more than a speck on the map; it is a cradle of culture, a testament to resilience, and a place where every rock, every wave, and every story carries meaning. It is a place that has shaped who I am and continues to influence how I see the world.

In this chapter, I hope to share with you not just the facts about American Samoa, but the spirit of the place that has shaped me. I want you to feel the sun on your skin, smell the salt in the air, and understand the depth of connection to a land that is more than just home—it is part of our very being.

QUOTABLES FROM THIS SECTION

> *"Culture is the compass that guides us in our decisions, actions, and relationships."*
>
> *"The 'fa'a Samoa' teaches us to navigate life with humility, grace, and a spirit of service."*
>
> *"To honor our ancestors is to live with integrity and purpose."*

Discussion questions

1. How does the concept of 'fa'a Samoa' (the Samoan way) compare to your cultural values or traditions?

   _____
   _____
   _____
   _____

2. In what ways do you see respect, humility, and community playing a role in your life?

   _____
   _____
   _____
   _____

3. How can you incorporate the lessons of honoring ancestors and cultural heritage into your modern life?

   _____
   _____
   _____
   _____

TONY SOLAITA LITTLE LEAGUE

"Do not let what you cannot do interfere with what you can do." — John Wooden

In American Samoa, baseball is more than just a game—it's a bridge between generations, a school of life, and a testament to the legacy of one man: Tony Solaita. Tony was the first Major League Baseball player to hail from American Samoa.

His name resonates across the islands, not just for his athletic achievements but for his deep commitment to his community. Over his career, Tony played for teams like the Kansas City Royals, Minnesota Twins, New York Yankees, and later in the Japanese league with the Nippon-Ham Fighters. But it was his return to the islands that left an indelible mark.

With a passion for nurturing young talent and sharing his love for the game, Tony founded the American Samoa Little League Association in the 1980s. He saw baseball as a way to teach discipline, teamwork, and resilience—values deeply rooted in our culture.

He dedicated himself to developing a baseball program that would not only sharpen players' skills on the field but also mold them into confident and principled individuals ready to take on life's challenges.

The Little League program that Tony started was about more than just learning how to hit a fastball or field a grounder. It was about learning how to handle failure with grace, how to celebrate success with humility, and how to carry oneself with the pride and dignity of a Samoan warrior.

I was fortunate to have the opportunity to play in Tony Solaita's Little League program. From a young age, I was captivated by the game and worked tirelessly to hone my skills, hoping to one day walk in Tony's footsteps.

I still remember one of my first games when I was eight years old. Tony himself was the main umpire that day, standing tall behind the pitcher's mound. The field was still new, with more rocks than grass in the infield. A line drive was hit right at me, playing shortstop.

I bent down to field it, but the ball hit a rock and shot straight up, smashing into my chin. Pain shot through me, and tears welled up in my eyes. Still, I found the ball, threw it to first base, and got the out. Tony walked over, put his hand on my shoulder, and said, "Only warriors make that play, son. And you're a warrior. But remember, warriors don't cry."

That moment left a lasting impression on me. It wasn't just about the pain or the play—it was about the mindset Tony was trying to instill in us. He taught us that life, like baseball, would throw us curveballs. There would be bad hops and unexpected challenges, but with the heart of a warrior, we could handle anything.

Tony's influence extended beyond the field. He was a mentor who cared deeply about the young players he coached. He wanted us to succeed in baseball, yes, but more importantly, he wanted us to succeed in life.

Under his guidance, the Little League program grew, and it began to produce a number of talented players who would go on to play at higher levels. His legacy lives on through the

American Samoa Baseball Association and Little League Baseball program, which continue to thrive today.

Reflecting on my time in Tony's program, I realize that the lessons I learned on those rocky fields were foundational to who I am today. Through the discipline of baseball, I developed a work ethic that I carried into my academic pursuits and later into my professional career.

It was in this environment that I learned the value of perseverance, teamwork, and the importance of community—values that are central to the Samoan way of life.

Years later, while playing for the American Samoa National Baseball Team at the Olympic qualifiers in Australia, I was recruited to play for Spring Arbor University in Michigan. I received a full baseball and academic scholarship, which set me on a new path.

But no matter where I went—from the fields of Michigan to coaching tours across Europe—I carried Tony's teachings with me. The courage, resilience, and pride he instilled in us on those diamond fields of American Samoa became the bedrock of my life.

Tony Solaita may no longer be with us, but his spirit is alive and well in every young player who steps up to bat, in every coach who invests in their community, and in every individual who remembers that a warrior's heart is forged in both victory and adversity.

His legacy isn't just in the records he set or the teams he played for; it's in the lives he touched and the lessons he passed down to generations of Samoan youth, including me.

QUOTABLES FROM THIS SECTION

> *"Life, like baseball, will throw you curveballs. Only with the heart of a warrior can you handle anything."*
>
> *"The lessons learned on the field are the same ones we carry into life: resilience, humility, and perseverance."*
>
> *"A warrior's heart is forged in both victory and adversity."*

DISCUSSION QUESTIONS

1. What life lessons have you learned from sports or other group activities? How have they shaped your character?

   _____
   _____
   _____
   _____

2. How does the concept of "playing with the heart of a warrior" apply to your approach to challenges?

   _____
   _____
   _____

   Discuss the importance of having role models like Tony Solaita in your community. Who are your role models, and why?

   _____
   _____
   _____

IMPORTANCE OF CULTURAL HERITAGE

"Culture is the widening of the mind and of the spirit." — Jawaharlal Nehru

Your cultural heritage is more than just the traditions, customs, beliefs, values, and practices passed down through generations. It is the essence of who you are, the story of where you come from, and a powerful anchor that keeps you grounded amid life's ever-changing tides.

Embracing your cultural heritage helps shape your identity, provides a sense of belonging, and guides you in making meaningful decisions throughout your life.

Understanding your heritage is like uncovering a treasure chest filled with wisdom and insight. It connects you to your ancestors and roots you in a community that has thrived on shared values and collective strength. When you know where you come from, you carry within you the strength of all who came before you—their struggles, their triumphs, and their wisdom.

Growing up in a culture that emphasizes respect for elders, authority, and the environment, I learned early on that heritage isn't just about the past; it's about how the past informs the present and shapes the future.

It is the foundation upon which we build our lives, influencing our values, beliefs, and how we perceive the world around us. In American Samoa, we were taught to see beyond ourselves, to recognize that each person is part of a larger tapestry woven with care, love, and respect.

Knowing your cultural heritage also allows you to appreciate the diversity of the world around you. It offers a deeper understanding of the differences between cultures and celebrates the uniqueness of each.

In a world that often emphasizes individualism, cultural heritage reminds us that we are part of something bigger—an intricate web of stories, traditions, and values that shape our identity and our place in the world.

More than that, embracing your heritage can be a source of strength and resilience. It can provide you with a sense of pride and purpose to draw upon when times get tough.

When faced with challenges, it's often our connection to our roots that helps us stand firm and make decisions grounded in who we truly are. I have found that my heritage has served as a compass, guiding me when I felt lost and giving me courage when I felt unsure.

But understanding your cultural heritage is not just about knowing your history; it's about integrating that history into your daily life. It's about living in a way that honors your roots while also embracing growth and change. As we navigate life's challenges, our cultural values can serve as a moral compass, helping us to stay true to ourselves and make choices that align with our deepest beliefs.

For me, embracing my Samoan heritage has meant understanding the deep sense of responsibility that comes with it. It means valuing community over self, respecting others, and being a steward of the land and traditions that have been passed down to me.

It has also meant understanding that heritage is dynamic, not static. As I grow, so does my understanding of what it means to be a Samoan, an entrepreneur, and a father in today's world.

By embracing your cultural heritage, you gain a greater sense of self-awareness and a deeper connection to your values. It's about finding strength in your story and using it to navigate the complexities of life with authenticity and purpose.

When you stand on the foundation of your heritage, you not only honor the past, but you also carve a path forward for future generations.

I encourage you to explore your own heritage deeply, to understand it not just as a part of your history but as a living, evolving part of who you are. In doing so, you'll uncover a powerful resource that can help you navigate life's challenges and live in a way that is both rooted and resilient.

Quotables from this Section

> *"Your heritage is a treasure chest filled with wisdom, insight, and strength."*
>
> *"Embracing your culture means honoring your past while shaping your future."*
>
> *"Heritage is dynamic, not static; it grows as we grow."*

DISCUSSION QUESTIONS

1. What aspects of your cultural heritage do you find most empowering, and why?

   _____
   _____
   _____
   _____

2. How can understanding your heritage help you make better decisions in life?

   _____
   _____
   _____
   _____

3. Discuss ways in which cultural heritage can serve as a source of strength and resilience during difficult times.

   _____
   _____
   _____
   _____

EXTRACTING LIFE PRINCIPLES

"The unexamined life is not worth living." —
Socrates

The moment you decide to be authentic and fully present is the moment you align with your purpose and the universe's intent for you. Extracting life principles is about uncovering the core values, beliefs, and guiding tenets that shape your approach to life.

These principles provide clarity and direction, helping you set meaningful goals, make informed decisions, and face challenges with confidence. This process isn't about following a one-size-fits-all formula; it's about engaging in deep self-reflection, understanding your cultural heritage, and identifying what truly resonates with you.

To extract meaningful life principles, you need to look inward—digging into your experiences, values, and the cultural roots that ground you. Your culture and life experiences are like a wellspring from which you can draw timeless lessons and insights. Here are ten steps to guide you in this journey of self-discovery:

1. Be a Student of Yourself

The first step is to learn who you are at your core. This requires honest self-reflection and a willingness to explore both your strengths and areas for growth. Start by journaling your thoughts, emotions, and experiences regularly. Reflect on what moments in your life felt most authentic or transformative. What values were at play during these times? By understanding these key moments, you begin to uncover what truly drives you. This self-awareness is the foundation upon which your principles are built.

2. Seek Outside Perspectives

Sometimes, it's hard to see ourselves clearly. Engaging with those who know you well—family, friends, mentors—can provide valuable insights into how others perceive your strengths, values, and areas for growth. Conduct "interviews" with a few trusted people in your life, asking them to share candid feedback about what they see as your core strengths and areas for improvement. This process not only offers new perspectives but can also highlight recurring themes you may not have noticed. These external insights can be invaluable in refining your understanding of yourself.

3. Embrace Your Cultural Heritage

Your cultural heritage is a rich source of values and beliefs that can deeply influence your life principles. Reflect on the traditions, stories, and values passed down through your family and community. Consider how these elements have shaped your understanding of values like loyalty, humility, or perseverance.

For example, growing up in a community-oriented culture may have instilled in you the importance of collective well-being and service to others. Recognize these cultural influences and incorporate them into your life principles where they resonate.

4. Organize and Analyze Your Insights

Once you've gathered your reflections and external feedback, take time to organize this information. Look for patterns and common themes that consistently emerge. Are there values or beliefs that are repeatedly mentioned?

Are there strengths that others see in you that you might have overlooked? This step is crucial because it allows you to start forming a clearer picture of your foundational principles. Tools like mind maps, charts, or simple lists can help in categorizing and prioritizing these insights. The goal is to distill your experiences and feedback into a cohesive set of core values.

5. Identify Recurring Themes and Core Beliefs

As you analyze your insights, begin to identify recurring themes and core beliefs that stand out. These are the values that resonate most deeply with you and that you want to embody in your daily life.

Ask yourself: *What values or beliefs do I want to guide my actions and decisions? Which of these principles reflect who I am and who I want to become?* Aim to narrow your list down to 3-5 core principles that capture the essence of what matters most to you.

6. Craft Your Manifesto

Now that you have a clearer understanding of your core values, it's time to put them into a concise statement—a personal manifesto. Your manifesto is a declaration of what you stand for and what you strive to embody in your daily life.

Think of it as your north star, guiding you through both triumphs and challenges.

To write it, consider all aspects of your identity—your heritage, beliefs, passions, and the lessons life has taught you. Ensure it's authentic, actionable, and reflects the person you are and want to become. Keep it simple, clear, and inspiring, so it resonates with you and serves as a constant reminder of your mission.

7. Test Your Principles in Real Life

Having a set of principles is one thing; living by them is another. Begin by testing your principles in real-life situations. Pay attention to how they influence your decisions, actions, and interactions. Are they guiding you effectively?

Are there instances where you find it challenging to adhere to them? Use these experiences as opportunities to refine your understanding of your principles. Remember, the goal is not perfection but progress. Your principles should be flexible enough to guide you through different contexts while remaining true to your core values.

8. Commit to Memory and Practice

Knowing your principles is important, but to make them a living part of who you are, you must commit them to memory and practice them daily. Create reminders for yourself—post them on your mirror, write them in your journal, or set them as a phone background.

The goal is to internalize these values so they naturally guide your actions and decisions. Consider starting each day with a brief reflection on your principles and how you will apply them. The more you practice aligning your decisions with your core values, the more they become second nature.

9. Normalize the Mission

Make your principles a natural part of your daily routine. This could be as simple as setting a daily intention based on your manifesto or reflecting at the end of the day on how you lived up to your values.

Surround yourself with people who support and reflect these values, fostering an environment where growth and authenticity are encouraged. Build rituals that remind you of your principles, like a morning meditation or a weekly review. Normalizing your mission means making these principles an automatic part of your mindset and behaviors.

10. Revisit and Evolve Your Principles Over Time

Life is dynamic, and so are you. As you grow and encounter new experiences, your understanding of your principles may deepen, and new values may emerge. Make it a habit to revisit your principles periodically—perhaps every year or after significant life events.

Reflect on whether they still resonate with who you are becoming. Ask yourself: *Are my current principles still aligned with my values and goals? Do they need to be refined or expanded?* Being open to evolving your principles is a sign of growth and wisdom.

By following these steps, you are not just learning about yourself—you are actively shaping the person you want to be. Extracting life principles from your experiences and cultural heritage allows you to live more intentionally and purposefully.

It's a journey that requires patience, reflection, and honesty, but the rewards—a life lived in alignment with who you truly are—are well worth it. Remember, your principles are not set in stone; they are living guides that grow with you as you continue to discover your true self.

Quotables from this section

> "Your principles are the foundation upon which you build your life."

> "Be a student of yourself; self-awareness is the key to authenticity."

> "Life principles are not fixed; they evolve as we continue to discover who we are."

Discussion Questions

1. What are some of your core life principles? How did you come to define them?

2. How can being a "student of yourself" lead to personal growth?

3. Discuss the importance of having a living set of principles that evolve over time. How do you ensure your principles stay relevant?

BE A STUDENT OF YOURSELF

"Knowing yourself is the beginning of all wisdom." — *Aristotle*

No one knows you better than you do—or at least, that's how it should be. To navigate life's challenges with clarity and purpose, you must become a lifelong student of yourself.

This means committing to a process of ongoing self-reflection, examining your thoughts, behaviors, values, and experiences to understand who you are at your core. It's about delving deeper into what drives you, where your strengths lie, and where there are opportunities for growth.

Start with Intentional Journaling

One of the most effective tools for self-discovery is journaling. This isn't just about writing down what happened during your day; it's about exploring your inner world—your thoughts, emotions, fears, and aspirations. Set aside time each day or week to reflect on key questions like:

- *What moments today felt most authentic to me?*
- *What situations triggered strong emotions, and why?*
- *Where did I feel most aligned with my values?*

Journaling creates a safe space for you to be completely honest with yourself without fear of judgment. It allows you to track your growth over time and see patterns in your behavior and thought processes.

Recognize Patterns and Themes

As you write, you will start to notice recurring themes in your entries. Perhaps you see a pattern where you feel most fulfilled when helping others, or a tendency to react defensively in certain situations. Recognizing these patterns is crucial because they reveal both your strengths and your areas for growth. For example:

- You may find that you are often drawn to creative problem-solving, which could be a sign to lean more into roles or projects that harness this strength.

- Conversely, identifying a pattern of avoiding difficult conversations might indicate an area where you could develop more courage or communication skills.

Engage in Self-Reflection Practices

Beyond journaling, engaging in other forms of self-reflection—like meditation, prayer, or spending time in nature—can provide clarity. These practices help you slow down and tune into your inner voice.

For instance, I found my own quiet space growing up in Samoa, hiking up to a waterfall after Sunday church services. I'd sit there with my little boom box, playing music, and let my thoughts flow. It was my time to talk to myself, to God, and to the world around me.

I would reflect on what I was feeling, who I was mad at, who I had a crush on, and everything in between. Those moments of solitude taught me to listen to myself and gave me a foundation of self-awareness that I still rely on today.

Analyze and Reflect on Your Findings

Periodically, go back and read your journal entries. Take note of what stands out—what insights have you gained about yourself?

- What patterns do you notice, and how do they align with your goals and values?

- Are there recurring emotions or reactions that indicate unresolved issues or areas that need attention?

Analyzing your reflections over time helps you see how you've evolved and where you might still be stuck. This deeper analysis enables you to identify specific areas for personal development.

Experiment with New Practices and Habits

Once you've identified patterns and areas for growth, commit to experimenting with new habits or practices that address these insights.

- If you notice that you're most energized when creating, dedicate more time each week to creative activities—whether it's writing, designing, or problem-solving.

- If you discover that anxiety or fear holds you back from pursuing certain goals, consider exploring mindfulness techniques or working with a coach or therapist to develop strategies for managing those fears.

Reflective Homework

If you have journaled in the past, take the next week to revisit your entries. Look for patterns or tendencies in your thoughts, behaviors, and emotions. If you haven't journaled recently, start today. Write every day for the next seven days, then return to these entries on the eighth day to reflect and assess. Your goal is to uncover insights that will help you become more actively involved in shaping your story.

PRO TIP: Before you write, take a moment to ground yourself. Offer a prayer, set an intention, or simply take a few deep breaths to center your mind. Acknowledge that this process is about discovery, growth, and grace—both for yourself and others. This mindset will help you approach journaling with openness and curiosity, allowing deeper truths to emerge.

Seek Outside Perspectives to Complement Your Self-Reflection

While being a student of yourself involves deep introspection, remember that we often have blind spots when it comes to our own growth. Sharing some of your reflections with a trusted friend or mentor can provide additional insights.

They may notice strengths or habits that you've overlooked or provide constructive feedback on areas you may want to explore further. This complementary perspective helps ensure that your self-study is well-rounded and grounded in reality.

Commit to a Journey of Authentic Growth

By committing to being a student of yourself, you are taking the most important step toward living authentically and purposefully. This journey of self-discovery is ongoing, and the more you embrace it, the more aligned you will become with who you truly are and who you're meant to be.

Remember, the goal is not perfection, but continuous growth and alignment with your true self.

Quotables from this section

> "To navigate life's challenges with clarity and purpose, you must first know yourself."

> "Self-reflection is the mirror that reveals our true selves."

> "Continuous self-discovery is the path to living authentically."

DISCUSSION QUESTIONS

1. What self-reflection practices have you found helpful in understanding who you are?

2. How do you balance self-awareness with self-compassion when identifying areas for growth?

3. What patterns have you noticed in your behavior or decision-making that align or conflict with your values?

INTERVIEW OTHERS ABOUT YOU

"We all need people who will give us feedback. That's how we improve." — *Bill Gates*

The best feedback is direct feedback, especially if it's from people who can be honest with you. While self-reflection is a powerful tool for self-discovery, sometimes the most valuable insights come from those who see us from the outside.

Interviewing others about yourself is a transformative exercise—it opens your eyes to both your blind spots and your unique strengths. However, this process requires humility, courage, and a genuine desire to grow. It's about seeking the truth with an open heart and a readiness to learn.

Why Seek Feedback from Others?

The people closest to you—family, friends, mentors, and colleagues—have witnessed you in various contexts. They've seen you in moments of triumph and in times of challenge.

They've observed how you handle stress, how you interact with others, and where your natural strengths and weaknesses lie. By engaging them in honest conversations, you invite them to share their perspectives on who you are and how you show up in the world.

Step 1: Choose a Diverse Group of People

Start by identifying 5-10 people who know you well and whose opinions you value. Make sure they represent different aspects of your life—family members, close friends, professional colleagues, mentors, or even past teachers or coaches.

A diverse group will provide a well-rounded view of your strengths and areas for improvement. Remember, the goal is to get a balanced perspective, not just to hear what you want to hear.

Key Tip: Ensure diversity in your group to gain a comprehensive understanding of how you are perceived in different contexts.

Step 2: Prepare Thoughtful, Open-Ended Questions

To gain meaningful insights, ask questions that encourage reflection. Instead of vague questions like "What do you think of me?" aim for questions that prompt deeper responses. Consider asking:

- *What do you see as my greatest strengths, and why?*

- *Are there any areas where you think I could grow or improve?*

- *Can you share a time when you saw me at my best? What qualities stood out to you?*

- *What patterns have you noticed in my behavior that could be holding me back?*

The key is to ask questions that open up space for honest dialogue. You want them to feel comfortable sharing both positive feedback and constructive criticism.

Key Tip: Open-ended questions lead to richer, more insightful feedback.

Step 3: Listen Actively and Without Judgment

When you engage in these conversations, approach them with curiosity, not defensiveness. Your role is to listen actively—focus on what is being said rather than formulating a response. Take notes or, if they're comfortable, record the conversation.

Pay attention to recurring themes, powerful words, or examples they use to describe you. These often hold the most valuable insights. Remember, the goal is growth, not validation.

Key Tip: Listening actively and without judgment fosters a safe environment for honest feedback.

Step 4: Reflect on a Personal Experience

Reflecting on feedback can be a deeply personal process. I recall one summer when I returned to Samoa, where I decided to embrace this process.

While my primary purpose was to work with the kids in Tony Solaita's Little League program and practice with our National

Baseball Team, I took the opportunity to have meaningful conversations with some of my elders and family members. I pulled a few aside and asked them about their lives, their perceptions of me, and any advice they had for my journey ahead.

Their responses ranged from light-hearted advice like my uncle's classic "eat more!" to more profound reflections about my character, work ethic, and how they saw my potential.

One of my older aunties, who thought I played in the NFL (I was a baseball player), told me that she was proud of my accomplishments and that I was a "good boy" who always remembered where he came from.

Her words, although simple, reminded me of the importance of staying grounded and connected to my roots, no matter where life takes me. These conversations were more than just feedback—they were moments of connection, learning, and self-awareness that added depth to my understanding of myself.

Key Tip: Personal stories can provide context and depth to the feedback you receive, making it more meaningful.

Step 5: Organize and Analyze the Feedback

After collecting the feedback, take time to sit with it. Look for patterns in what people have said.

- Are there strengths or areas of improvement that multiple people have mentioned?

- Do the insights align with your self-perception, or do they challenge you in ways you hadn't considered before?

Reflecting on these patterns will help you gain a more rounded and objective view of yourself. This analysis will enable you to see where your growth opportunities lie and where your natural strengths can be leveraged further.

Key Tip: Analyzing feedback helps transform raw insights into actionable personal growth.

Step 6: Turn Insights into Actionable Steps

The purpose of gathering feedback is to grow. For each theme or recurring feedback point, identify at least one actionable step. For example:

- If several people mention that you have a tendency to avoid conflict, a step could be to practice having difficult conversations in low-stakes settings or to seek guidance from a mentor on assertive communication.

- If you're praised for being a great listener but lack assertiveness, consider a public speaking class to build confidence in expressing your views.

These tangible steps will help you transform insights into meaningful growth.

Key Tip: Turning feedback into concrete actions is key to personal development.

Reflective Homework

Identify 5-10 people who can provide honest, constructive feedback about you. Arrange to meet with them and ask them the same set of questions.

Be sure to listen deeply and take notes. Afterward, review your notes carefully, highlighting key themes and insights. Reflect on what you've learned and consider how you can use this feedback to grow.

PRO TIP: Approach these conversations as a learner, not a judge. You're not looking to defend yourself; you're seeking to understand yourself better. The more open you are to receiving feedback, the more valuable it will be.

The Power of Feedback for Deeper Self-Awareness

By interviewing others about yourself, you open the door to deeper self-awareness. This process not only helps you recognize your strengths but also illuminates the areas where you can evolve. Remember, growth begins with understanding.

Embrace the insights, take actionable steps, and continue to seek feedback regularly. The more open you are to learning from others, the more aligned you will become with your true self.

Quotables from this section

"Feedback is a gift; it shows us who we are and who we can become."

"We all have blind spots; sometimes, it takes others to help us see them."

"Growth begins with understanding, and understanding starts with listening."

Discussion questions

1. How does seeking feedback from others provide a different perspective on who you are?

   _____
   _____
   _____

2. Discuss a time when feedback from someone else led to a significant change in your life. What did you learn?

   _____
   _____
   _____

3. What are some challenges you might face when asking for honest feedback, and how can you overcome them?

   _____
   _____
   _____

ORGANIZE THE DATA

"Data is a precious thing and will last longer than the systems themselves." — Tim Berners-Lee

There is no substitute for organized data. The more organized you are, the closer you are to living your best life.

Collecting insights from your self-reflection and interviews is a valuable step in understanding yourself better, but without proper organization, these insights can become overwhelming or lose their effectiveness.

The next crucial step in your journey of self-discovery is to systematically organize this data. By doing so, you can identify patterns, extract key themes, and turn these insights into meaningful, actionable guidance.

Step 1: Start by Categorizing Your Data

Begin by sorting your notes from your journaling and interviews into categories. This could be by themes such as "Leadership," "Communication," "Resilience," or "Empathy." The goal here is to group similar feedback and reflections together so you can see where there is alignment and where there might be contradictions. For example:

- If multiple people mentioned your ability to stay calm under pressure, that could fall under a category like "Composure."

- Conversely, if feedback highlighted a need to improve directness in communication, you might create a category labeled "Assertiveness."

Key Tip: Categorizing your data helps you see a clearer picture of recurring themes in your strengths and areas for development.

Step 2: Look for Patterns and Key Insights

As you categorize the data, pay attention to recurring themes and insights. Are there certain strengths or growth areas that keep coming up? These patterns are significant—they highlight the core attributes that define you and the areas that need more focus. For example:

- You might notice a pattern where people see you as reliable but mention a tendency to avoid conflict. This suggests both a strength and an area for development.

Understanding these patterns allows you to see a fuller picture of how you show up in the world and where you might want to grow.

Key Tip: Identifying patterns helps you understand both your natural strengths and potential growth areas.

Step 3: Visualize the Information

Sometimes, seeing your data laid out visually can help make sense of it. Consider using tools like mind maps, flowcharts, or even digital tools like Trello or Miro to visually organize and connect themes.

This approach helps you spot relationships between different insights and makes it easier to identify areas for growth or development. For those who prefer a more structured approach, a spreadsheet can also be effective for categorizing feedback and tracking patterns.

During one of my visits back home, I applied this concept on a family project. We were mapping out our family tree, and what started as a simple task quickly became a more in-depth exploration of our family's history and relationships.

By organizing the data, we were able to uncover connections we hadn't considered before and see how our shared heritage shaped who we are. This process of organizing was crucial not just for clarity but for a deeper understanding of our roots.

Key Tip: Visualizing your data helps you make connections between insights and identify overarching themes.

Step 4: Create Summaries and Reflections for Each Theme

Once you've organized the feedback into categories, take the time to write a brief summary for each theme. Reflect on the most significant insights and consider how they align with your self-perception. Ask yourself:

- *Does this feedback resonate with how I see myself?*
- *What surprises me?*
- *What challenges my self-concept?*

These summaries help distill the feedback into key takeaways that can guide your growth.

Key Tip: Summarizing each theme allows you to distill complex feedback into focused insights for growth.

Step 5: Identify Actionable Steps for Each Insight

Organizing the data isn't just about understanding who you are—it's about using that understanding to grow. For each category or theme, identify at least one actionable step you can take to enhance a strength or address a development area. For example:

- If "Assertiveness" is a recurring theme, an actionable step might be to practice speaking up in meetings or to take a course on effective communication.

These tangible steps help turn feedback into growth opportunities.

Key Tip: Defining actionable steps turns raw insights into a structured roadmap for personal development.

Reflective Homework

Set aside time this week to organize your data. Choose a method that works best for you—whether it's a digital tool, a mind map, or a physical notebook.

Create categories, summarize key insights, and determine actionable steps. This exercise will help transform raw feedback into a structured roadmap for personal and professional development.

PRO TIP: Keep refining your categories and insights as you grow. The process of self-discovery is ongoing, and as you evolve, so will your understanding of the data. Periodically revisit this exercise to stay aligned with your growth journey.

The Importance of Organizing Insights for Growth

By organizing your insights effectively, you move from simply knowing yourself to actively shaping your growth path.

This process lays the foundation for developing a personal manifesto that aligns with your core values and aspirations. Organized data not only clarifies where you are but also points you in the direction of where you want to go.

Quotables from this section

> *"Data is powerful when it is organized and turned into actionable insights."*

> *"Look for patterns; they reveal both our strengths and areas for growth."*

> *"Visualizing your insights can help you make meaningful connections."*

DISCUSSION QUESTIONS

1. How can organizing insights from self-reflection and feedback help you create a clearer path for growth?

2. What tools or methods have you found effective in organizing your thoughts and plans?

3. Discuss the importance of recognizing patterns in your life and how they can guide future actions.

CRAFT YOUR MANIFESTO

Your life, your manifesto! Make it memorable.

Now that you have a clearer understanding of your core values, it's time to put them into a concise statement—a personal manifesto. Your manifesto is a declaration of what you stand for and what you strive to embody in your daily life.

Think of it as your North Star, guiding you through both triumphs and challenges. Crafting a manifesto is not just about writing a statement; it's about creating a living document that evolves with you as you grow.

Step 1: Reflect on Your Core Values and Beliefs

Start by reflecting on the core values and beliefs you've identified through self-reflection, feedback from others, and exploration of your cultural heritage. Think deeply about what each value means to you and why it's important.

Consider how these values have influenced your past decisions and how you want them to shape your future. Ask yourself: *What do I stand for? What principles do I want to guide my life?*

To get started, list down your top 3-5 values. For each one, write a few sentences about what it means to you. For example, if one of your values is "integrity," you might write, "Integrity means being honest and transparent in all my dealings, even when it's inconvenient or uncomfortable. It's about doing the right thing, even when no one is watching."

Key Takeaway: A strong manifesto starts with a deep understanding of your values and beliefs.

Step 2: Consider All Aspects of Your Identity

Your manifesto should reflect the entirety of who you are—your heritage, beliefs, passions, and the lessons life has taught you. Think about the different roles you play in life (e.g., leader, parent, partner, community member) and how your values manifest in each.

Consider the unique cultural or familial influences that have shaped you. How have these experiences contributed to your understanding of what matters most?

For instance, if your cultural heritage emphasizes community and collective well-being, this could be a central theme in your manifesto.

A statement like, "I commit to uplifting and supporting my community, honoring the values of collaboration and shared growth," captures both personal and cultural elements.

Key Takeaway: A holistic manifesto incorporates all dimensions of your identity, creating a more authentic and comprehensive declaration of who you are.

Step 3: Draft Your Manifesto in Clear, Concise Language

When drafting your manifesto, aim for clarity and brevity. Use simple, powerful language that resonates with you. Your manifesto should be easy to remember and recite, so avoid lengthy or complex sentences. Focus on what you want to embody in your daily actions. A well-crafted manifesto might look something like this:

- *"I commit to living with integrity, leading with empathy, and striving for growth every day. I will embrace challenges as opportunities to learn and will uplift others by being a source of encouragement and support."*

Remember, your manifesto doesn't have to be long to be meaningful. A few well-chosen words can have a profound impact.

Key Takeaway: Keep your manifesto concise and clear, making it easy to internalize and live by.

Step 4: Use a Manifesto Checklist to Ensure Completeness

To ensure your manifesto is both comprehensive and actionable, use a checklist to guide you. Here's a simple checklist to help you craft your manifesto:

- Does it reflect my core values and beliefs?
- Is it written in clear and simple language?

- Does it encompass all aspects of my identity (personal, cultural, professional)?

- Is it specific enough to guide my daily actions?

- Is it inspiring and motivating for me to read and reflect on?

By reviewing your manifesto against these criteria, you ensure it serves as a powerful guide for your life.

Key Takeaway: A manifesto checklist helps you create a statement that is not only authentic but also practical and motivating.

Step 5: Test and Refine Your Manifesto Over Time

A manifesto is not a static document; it evolves as you grow. Once you've drafted your manifesto, live with it for a while. Place it somewhere visible—on your desk, in your journal, or on a wall where you'll see it daily.

Reflect on it regularly and notice how it feels. Does it still resonate with you after a few weeks or months? Are there any parts that feel incomplete or need adjustment?

I remember drafting my first manifesto and feeling proud of it, but after a few months, I realized that some parts no longer fully captured my evolving values. I refined it to better reflect where I was in my journey, making it more relevant and powerful.

Key Takeaway: Regularly revisit and refine your manifesto to ensure it remains aligned with your evolving self.

Potential Challenge: Feeling like your manifesto isn't "perfect" right away. **Solution:** Embrace the idea that it's a living document and allow it to evolve naturally.

Step 6: Share Your Manifesto and Seek Feedback

Sharing your manifesto with trusted friends, mentors, or peers can provide valuable feedback and additional perspectives. This process not only helps refine your manifesto but also holds you accountable. When others know what you stand for, they can support you in living up to those standards.

For example, when I shared my manifesto with a close friend, she offered insights into how I could make it more specific and actionable. This feedback was invaluable in creating a more powerful and effective manifesto.

Key Takeaway: Feedback can help refine your manifesto and ensure it resonates with both you and those who know you well.

Potential Challenge: Fear of judgment or criticism. **Solution:** Share with individuals who respect and support your journey.

Step 7: Use Your Manifesto as a Daily Guide

Your manifesto should serve as a daily guide, helping you navigate decisions and challenges. Start each day by reading your manifesto and setting an intention based on it.

Use it as a framework for making decisions, especially when faced with difficult choices. Ask yourself: *Does this action align with my manifesto? Does it reflect who I want to be?*

When I began using my manifesto as a guide, it helped me stay focused on my core values, especially during times of stress or uncertainty. It became a touchstone that reminded me of what truly mattered.

Key Takeaway: A manifesto is most powerful when used as a daily guide to navigate life's complexities.

Potential Challenge: Forgetting to use your manifesto as a guide. **Solution:** Incorporate it into your morning or evening routine to keep it top of mind.

Your Homework

Set aside 30 minutes this week to draft your personal manifesto using the checklist provided. Share your first draft with someone you trust and ask for feedback. Revisit and refine your manifesto over the next month, adjusting it as needed until it fully resonates with you.

PRO TIP: Think of your manifesto as a compass—always there to guide you, but adjustable as you discover new paths. Keep it visible, keep it evolving, and let it lead you toward your most authentic self.

By crafting a personal manifesto, you create a powerful tool that not only captures who you are but also guides you in becoming who you want to be. It is a declaration of your commitment to living a life of purpose, integrity, and authenticity.

Quotables from this Section

> *"Your manifesto is your North Star; let it guide you in every decision and action."*

> *"A strong manifesto reflects your values, beliefs, and unique identity."*

> *"A manifesto is a living document, meant to evolve as you do."*

Discussion Questions

1. What would you include in your personal manifesto? Why are these values or beliefs important to you?

2. How can having a personal manifesto help you navigate tough decisions?

3. Discuss the process of creating a manifesto. How might it evolve as you grow and change?

OVERCOMING SETBACKS

"Success is not final, failure is not fatal: It is the courage to continue that counts." — Winston S. Churchill

Life will inevitably throw curveballs our way—moments of unexpected setbacks, failures, and challenges that test our resolve. Defining your life principles is a powerful step, but living by them day in and day out is where the real challenge lies.

Staying committed to your principles isn't always straightforward. There will be times when obstacles, failures, or unforeseen circumstances test your resolve. It's during these moments that your principles are truly put to the test.

But here's the truth: setbacks are not signs of failure; they are natural parts of the growth process. Each challenge you face is an opportunity to strengthen your commitment to your principles or to reassess and refine them.

When we see setbacks as stepping stones rather than stumbling blocks, we unlock the power of transformation. The key is to recognize setbacks as moments of learning rather than moments of defeat. Ask yourself:

- *What can I learn from this experience?*

- *How can I use this challenge to reinforce my values or adjust my approach?*

Personal Story: Reframing Challenges on the Field and in Life

When I was coaching baseball in Europe, we faced a particularly tough season where our team lost more games than we won. It would have been easy to abandon our core principles of teamwork and resilience.

Instead, we took a step back, reassessed our strategies, and used each loss as an opportunity to learn and grow. We didn't see those losses as failures; we saw them as lessons. We adapted our approach to address the challenges we hadn't anticipated, coming back stronger both as a team and as individuals.

That season taught me that growth often comes when we lean into discomfort and use it as a catalyst for change.

Your Resilience Toolkit: Practical Steps to Navigate Setbacks

To navigate setbacks effectively, it's essential to have a set of tools that help you stay grounded, focused, and ready to adapt. Here's a resilience toolkit to guide you through the toughest times:

1. **Setback Analysis Worksheet:** After facing a setback, take the time to conduct a detailed analysis. Write down the situation, the emotions you felt, the decisions you made, and what you learned from it. This exercise will help you approach future challenges with more wisdom and confidence.

2. **Grounding Rituals:** Create personal rituals that help you stay anchored in your core values during difficult times. This could be a morning meditation, a nature walk, or journaling about your principles and why they

matter. For me, it's revisiting the teachings and values from my Samoan heritage—principles like respect, humility, and community that have been my anchor in turbulent times.

3. **Mindset Shift Exercises:** Practice reframing your thoughts. Instead of thinking, "Why is this happening to me?" try asking, "What is this teaching me?" This simple shift in mindset can turn a disempowering situation into an empowering one, reminding you that growth often comes through discomfort.

4. **Visualize the Lesson Learned:** Imagine yourself in the situation where the setback occurred, and visualize how you would handle it differently based on what you've learned. This exercise solidifies the lessons in your mind and prepares you for future challenges.

5. **Support Network Check-In:** Surround yourself with resilient influences—mentors, friends, or communities who understand the importance of growth and adaptation. Schedule regular check-ins with these individuals to discuss challenges, receive support, and gain new perspectives. They can offer encouragement

when you're down and challenge you when you're stuck.

Adapting Without Losing Your Essence

Adapting doesn't mean abandoning your principles; it means finding new ways to live them in changing circumstances. Sometimes, a principle may need to be reframed or adjusted to fit a new context. This requires flexibility and an open mind. Ask yourself:

- *Is this principle still serving me well in this situation?*
- *How can I adapt it to be more effective while staying true to my core values?*

Think of adaptation like a tree bending in the wind. It doesn't break; it adjusts its shape to withstand the storm. In the same way, your principles can bend and flex without breaking. They can evolve as you grow and as life presents new challenges.

Broader Perspective: Learning from Others' Setbacks

It's not just our stories that shape us; it's also the stories of others. A coaching colleague of mine once faced a major setback when he lost his position as head coach.

Rather than seeing it as the end of his career, he analyzed what went wrong, sought feedback from his players, and focused on improving his communication and trust-building skills. He returned to coaching with a renewed sense of purpose and more effective strategies, reminding us that setbacks can be turning points if we are willing to learn from them.

Reaffirm Your Commitment to Your Principles

After adapting your approach and learning from setbacks, it's important to reaffirm your commitment to your principles. Revisit them with a renewed sense of purpose, knowing that they are not just words on a page but living, evolving guides for your life.

This reaffirmation can be done through journaling, speaking them out loud as daily affirmations, or sharing them with a trusted friend or mentor who can hold you accountable.

Reflective Action Steps: Building Your Resilience

- **Reflect on a Recent Setback:** Think about a recent challenge you've faced. Write down what happened, how it made you feel, and what you learned from it.

- **Identify One Core Value to Reinforce:** Based on your reflection, choose one core value that you want to strengthen. Create an action plan for how you will live out this value more fully, especially in challenging situations.

- **Create Your Own Resilience Toolkit:** Develop a personal set of tools that help you navigate setbacks. Include rituals, mindset exercises, and support systems that align with your principles.

PRO TIP: Don't fear the process of adaptation. It doesn't mean you're giving up on your values; it means you're allowing them to grow with you. Stay flexible, stay grounded, and remember that each challenge is a chance to reaffirm who you are and what you stand for.

Embrace the Power of Resilience and Adaptation

By understanding that setbacks are part of the journey and that your principles can be adapted without losing their essence, you develop the resilience needed to live authentically.

Growth is not a straight path but a winding road filled with lessons that make you stronger, wiser, and more aligned with your true self.

Quotables from this section

> *"Setbacks are not signs of failure; they are opportunities for growth."*

> *"Adversity is the true test of your principles; let them bend but not break."*

> *"Resilience is about turning setbacks into stepping stones for future success."*

DISCUSSION QUESTIONS

1. Reflect on a recent setback you experienced. What did it teach you about yourself and your principles?

2. How can setbacks serve as opportunities for growth rather than moments of defeat?

3. What tools or practices do you use to stay resilient in the face of challenges?

COMMIT TO MEMORY AND PRACTICE

"We are what we repeatedly do. Excellence, then, is not an act, but a habit." — Aristotle

Knowing your principles is important, but making them a living part of who you are requires committing them to memory and practicing them consistently.

This process is about more than just memorization; it involves internalizing your values so they guide your actions naturally. The goal is to integrate these principles into your daily life until they become second nature.

Step 1: Use Visualization and Affirmations

Visualization is a powerful technique for internalizing your principles. Spend a few minutes each day visualizing scenarios where you apply your principles. Imagine yourself in challenging situations—how would you act if you were fully aligned with your principles?

How would it feel to make choices rooted in your deepest beliefs? Visualization helps create a mental blueprint for action, making it easier to live out your values when those situations arise in real life.

Affirmations are another effective tool. Start your day by stating your principles out loud, like a mantra. For example, if one of your principles is "lead with integrity," you might say, "Today, I will lead with integrity in every action and decision I make." Repeating these affirmations helps reinforce your commitment and keeps your principles at the forefront of your mind.

Key Takeaway: Visualization and affirmations help you mentally rehearse living by your principles, making it more likely you'll act in alignment with them.

Potential Challenge: It might feel awkward or forced initially.
Solution: Start with small, simple affirmations or visualizations and gradually build them into a comfortable daily habit.

Step 2: Create Daily Rituals Around Your Principles

Creating daily rituals can help anchor your principles into your everyday life. A ritual could be as simple as a morning meditation where you reflect on your values and set an intention for the day or a nightly journaling practice where you assess how well you lived up to your principles.

These rituals serve as reminders and provide a regular check-in to keep you aligned with your mission.

For instance, a friend of mine created a "values moment" during her lunch break each day, where she reviews her top three principles and reflects on how she has been living them out so far. This daily ritual has helped her stay centered and purposeful throughout the day, even amidst a busy schedule.

Key Takeaway: Rituals reinforce your principles by making them a regular, habitual part of your routine.

Potential Challenge: It can be easy to skip rituals when life gets busy. **Solution:** Start small, make them enjoyable, and tie them to existing habits (like journaling with your morning coffee).

Step 3: Use Visual Reminders to Keep Principles Top of Mind

Visual reminders can be powerful in helping you remember and live by your principles. Write your principles down and place them in locations where you'll see them often—on your bathroom mirror, as the wallpaper on your phone, or on a sticky note on your computer.

The goal is to have constant reminders that reinforce these values throughout your day. Consider creating a vision board that incorporates your principles with images and quotes that inspire you.

I keep a card in my wallet with my key principles written on it. This simple act ensures that whenever I reach for my wallet, I'm reminded of the commitments I've made to myself. It's a small practice, but it makes a big difference in staying grounded in what truly matters.

Key Takeaway: Visual cues keep your principles visible and accessible, making it harder to forget them.

Potential Challenge: Visual reminders can become "background noise" over time. **Solution:** Change the location or format of your reminders periodically to keep them fresh and noticeable.

Step 4: Set Up Regular Reflection Sessions

Reflection is key to ensuring that your principles remain relevant and impactful. At the end of each day or week, take a few moments to reflect on how you've embodied your principles. Ask yourself: *Did I live in alignment with my values today?*

Where did I succeed, and where did I fall short? This reflection helps you stay accountable and identify areas where you need to be more mindful. Over time, this practice not only strengthens your commitment but also allows your principles to evolve as needed.

I conduct a "principle reflection" every Sunday evening, where I assess my week and write about specific moments where I applied my principles and where I may have deviated. This reflection allows me to course-correct and re-commit for the week ahead.

Key Takeaway: Regular reflection sessions help you stay aligned with your principles and adapt them as necessary.

Potential Challenge: Forgetting to reflect or not knowing what to focus on. **Solution:** Schedule a fixed time for reflection and use prompts to guide your thoughts (e.g., "What challenges did I face in living by my principles this week?").

Step 5: Share Your Principles with Others for Accountability

Sharing your principles with trusted friends, family, or mentors adds another layer of accountability. When you articulate your principles to others, you reinforce them for yourself. Moreover, those who know your values can help remind you of them when you stray.

Consider sharing your principles in conversations, using them as a framework for decision-making discussions, or even incorporating them into team or family agreements.

For example, I shared my principles with my team and my family. It wasn't about imposing my values on them, but rather about creating a shared understanding of what drives me. In doing so, I found that others often held me accountable to those standards, which further reinforced my commitment.

Key Takeaway: Sharing your principles creates external accountability, making it more likely you will adhere to them.

Potential Challenge: Fear of being judged or misunderstood. **Solution:** Share with trusted individuals who respect and support your growth journey.

Step 6: Teach Your Principles to Reinforce Learning

One of the most powerful ways to commit principles to memory is to teach them to others. Whether it's sharing with a friend, leading a workshop, or mentoring someone, teaching forces you to articulate your understanding clearly and helps reinforce your own learning. It also deepens your commitment because you are now responsible for embodying what you teach.

When I mentor young leaders, I often teach them the principles of resilience and integrity by sharing how these values have shaped my decisions. Not only does this help them, but it also serves as a constant reminder for me to live by these same principles.

Key Takeaway: Teaching is a powerful form of learning that solidifies your commitment to your principles.

Potential Challenge: Teaching can be intimidating if you feel you're not "perfect" in living by your principles. **Solution:** Embrace imperfection and teach from a place of honesty and growth.

Your Homework

Choose one or two methods—visualization, affirmations, rituals, visual reminders, reflection, sharing with others, or teaching—that you will use to commit your principles to memory over the next month. Track your progress and note any changes you observe in how you embody your principles.

PRO TIP: Commit to a 30-day challenge where you practice at least one method daily. Consistency is key to turning principles into habits.

By committing your principles to memory and integrating them into your daily life, you move from merely knowing your values to living them. This practice creates a strong foundation for authenticity, guiding you to make decisions that are true to who you are, even in the face of challenges.

Quotables from this Section

> "We are what we repeatedly do. Make excellence a habit, not an act."

> "Daily rituals reinforce our principles and keep us aligned with our mission."

> "Reflect regularly; it helps you stay true to your values and adapt when needed."

Discussion questions

1. How do daily rituals or habits help reinforce your principles and values?

2. What are some effective ways to integrate your principles into your daily life?

3. Discuss the importance of reflection and adjustment when your actions don't align with your values.

BUILDING A SUPPORT SYSTEM

"Surround yourself with only people who are going to lift you higher." — Oprah Winfrey

Living by your principles and staying true to your mission is not a solo journey. While self-reflection, commitment, and adaptation are crucial, the people you surround yourself with play an equally important role.

Building a support system of like-minded individuals, mentors, and communities who encourage your growth and hold you accountable can make all the difference in staying on track and continuing to evolve.

Step 1: Identify the Right People for Your Inner Circle

Not everyone in your life will understand or support your mission. That's why it's important to be intentional about who you invite into your inner circle. Seek out people who share similar values or have a growth mindset.

These individuals don't have to agree with you on everything, but they should challenge you to be better, hold you accountable to your principles, and support you in living authentically. Your inner circle might include close friends, family members, mentors, colleagues, or even like-minded peers from various communities.

Reflect on who has played a positive role in your life. Who inspires you? Who encourages you to think bigger, to act with integrity, or to stay committed to your growth? These are the people you want in your corner.

Transition to Next Step: Building your inner circle is just the beginning; creating spaces where these relationships can thrive is equally important.

Step 2: Find and Engage with Communities That Align with Your Values

Beyond your immediate circle, look for communities—both online and offline—that align with your values and principles.

This could be a professional group, a spiritual community, a mastermind group, or a local club.

Engaging with such communities provides a platform for sharing ideas, learning from others, and finding support. These communities can offer diverse perspectives, help you navigate challenges, and provide encouragement when you face setbacks.

I remember finding a community of fellow coaches who were also committed to personal development and authentic leadership. Their support was invaluable as we shared our experiences, challenges, and wins. Knowing that others were on a similar journey provided strength and motivation to keep pushing forward.

Key Takeaway: A strong community can serve as a wellspring of motivation and resilience, helping you stay true to your mission.

Potential Challenge: It can be daunting to find the right community. **Solution:** Start by attending events, webinars, or workshops that interest you and gradually build connections from there.

Step 3: Be Intentional About Building Relationships with Mentors

Mentors can be invaluable in your journey of living by your principles. They have often walked the path before you, faced similar challenges, and have wisdom to share. Seek out mentors who embody the qualities you aspire to have and who have successfully navigated the challenges you are facing.

Don't be afraid to reach out, ask questions, and build a genuine connection. A mentor's guidance can help you see blind spots, stay focused on your goals, and make informed decisions.

Early in my career, I had a mentor who always emphasized the importance of "servant leadership"—leading by example and putting the team first. His guidance shaped my approach to coaching and leadership. His support reminded me to stay humble, grounded, and always ready to learn from others.

Key Takeaway: A mentor provides not just advice but also accountability and encouragement, helping you stay committed to your growth.

Potential Challenge: Finding a good mentor who truly understands your journey can be challenging. **Solution:** Be clear about what you seek in a mentor and don't hesitate to approach multiple individuals until you find the right fit.

Step 4: Create Mutual Accountability Partnerships

Having an accountability partner can be a powerful way to stay committed to your principles. Find someone who is also on a journey of personal growth and create a mutual agreement to hold each other accountable.

This could involve regular check-ins, sharing goals, discussing setbacks, and celebrating progress together. Accountability partners provide a safe space for honest conversations and constructive feedback, helping you stay on track even when the going gets tough.

Consider forming a "Growth Circle" with a few trusted individuals where you meet monthly to share your progress, reflect on your experiences, and support each other's growth. This shared accountability fosters a sense of community and commitment that can keep you motivated.

Key Takeaway: Accountability partners create a structured environment for growth, providing both support and constructive feedback.

Potential Challenge: Maintaining consistency with accountability check-ins can be tough. **Solution:** Schedule these meetings in advance and treat them like important appointments.

Step 5: Cultivate an Environment that Reflects Your Values

Your environment plays a significant role in shaping your behavior and mindset. Surround yourself with positive influences—people who encourage growth, spaces that inspire creativity, and resources that align with your mission.

This might mean decluttering negative influences, both physically and mentally. An environment filled with supportive people, inspiring books, motivating visuals, and constructive conversations reinforces your commitment to your principles.

When I decided to focus more on personal development, I started attending workshops, reading books by inspiring leaders, and seeking out discussions that aligned with my values. This shift created an environment where growth felt natural and supported, rather than forced.

Key Takeaway: A supportive environment nurtures your growth and reinforces your commitment to your principles.

Potential Challenge: It can be difficult to change your environment if you're surrounded by negativity. **Solution:** Start by making small changes—introduce positive elements and gradually reduce negative influences.

Step 6: Be Willing to Evolve Your Support System

As you grow, your support needs will change. Some relationships will deepen, while others may no longer serve your evolving mission. Be willing to reassess your support system periodically. Ask yourself: *Is my current support network helping me grow, stay accountable, and live authentically? Are there new relationships I should cultivate or old ones that need to be reassessed?* A dynamic support system grows with you, adapting to your changing needs and goals.

During my most challenging times, I leaned on a network of mentors and peers who had faced their own setbacks and came out stronger. Their stories, guidance, and encouragement reminded me that the road to success is rarely a straight line. They inspired me to keep going, keep adapting, and keep growing.

Key Takeaway: A flexible support system is essential for long-term growth and adaptability.

Potential Challenge: Letting go of relationships that no longer serve you can be difficult. **Solution:** Focus on gratitude for what those relationships have given you and seek out new connections that align with your current goals.

Your Homework

Identify three people who could be part of your inner circle and three communities that align with your values. Reach out to one potential mentor this week and explore opportunities to engage more deeply with a community that supports your mission.

PRO TIP: Remember, the quality of your support system is more important than the quantity. Focus on cultivating meaningful, authentic relationships rather than just expanding your network. A few strong, supportive connections can have a greater impact than many superficial ones.

By building a support system that aligns with your principles, you create a foundation that not only supports your growth but also holds you accountable to the person you aspire to become. Your journey is yours to walk, but you don't have to walk it alone.

Quotables from this Section

> "You are the average of the five people you spend the most time with; choose wisely."

> "A strong support system is a foundation for growth, resilience, and accountability."

> "Surround yourself with those who lift you higher and challenge you to be better."

Discussion questions

1. Who are the people in your life that make up your support system? How do they contribute to your growth?

2. How can you build or strengthen a community that aligns with your values?

3. What role do mentors and accountability partners play in helping you stay true to your mission?

APPLYING PRINCIPLES IN DIFFERENT LIFE CONTEXTS

"In matters of style, swim with the current; in matters of principle, stand like a rock." — *Thomas Jefferson*

Your principles serve as the foundation for your life, but their true power is realized when they are actively applied across different areas of your life. Whether in your career, relationships, community, or personal growth, principles are meant to be lived.

Applying them in varied contexts not only reinforces your commitment to them but also deepens your understanding of what it means to live authentically.

Context 1: Career and Professional Life

Your professional life is one of the most significant arenas where your principles will be tested and refined. Applying your values in the workplace can guide your decisions, interactions, and approach to leadership.

For example, if one of your core principles is "integrity," you might make it a point to always be transparent with your colleagues and clients, even when it's difficult. This could mean owning up to a mistake rather than shifting blame or choosing to provide honest feedback rather than staying silent.

For instance, I remember a time when a client project I was leading faced significant delays due to unforeseen circumstances. Instead of downplaying the situation, I chose to communicate transparently with the client about the challenges we were facing and the steps we were taking to get back on track. This decision was not easy, but it aligned with my principle of integrity and ultimately strengthened the trust between us.

Key Takeaway: Living by your principles at work requires courage and consistency, but it builds a foundation of trust and respect.

Potential Challenge: Fear of backlash or negative consequences when being transparent. **Solution:** Weigh the long-term benefits of maintaining integrity over short-term discomfort. Communicate openly and focus on problem-solving.

Context 2: Relationships and Family Life

Relationships are where your principles often have the most immediate and visible impact. Whether it's with family, friends, or romantic partners, applying your values in these contexts requires intentionality and empathy.

For instance, if your principle is "active listening," this means making a conscious effort to be fully present during conversations with loved ones, setting aside distractions, and truly hearing what the other person is saying.

During a particularly heated family discussion about future plans, I reminded myself of my principle of "empathy before judgment." Instead of reacting defensively, I focused on listening and understanding the perspectives of others. This shift not only de-escalated the situation but also led to a more constructive and meaningful dialogue.

Key Takeaway: Applying principles like empathy, respect, and active listening in relationships helps build stronger, more authentic connections.

Potential Challenge: Emotional reactions can override principles. **Solution:** Practice mindfulness techniques to stay grounded and respond rather than react during conflicts.

Context 3: Community and Social Engagement

Your principles don't just guide your private life; they also shape how you engage with the community and the world around you.

Applying your values in social contexts could mean volunteering for causes that align with your beliefs, participating in local events that foster community growth, or advocating for issues that matter to you. If one of your principles is "service to others," consider finding ways to give back—whether through mentorship, charity work, or simply being a reliable, supportive friend in your circle.

For me, "community stewardship" is a principle that I live by. Growing up in a Samoan village, I learned that community is everything. I make it a point to be actively involved in community-building activities, whether it's coaching a local youth team or participating in neighborhood clean-up events. These actions are small but significant ways to honor my values and contribute to the well-being of those around me.

Key Takeaway: Applying principles in community engagement creates a ripple effect that encourages collective growth and positive impact.

Potential Challenge: Balancing community engagement with personal and professional responsibilities. **Solution:** Set realistic goals for your involvement and choose activities that align closely with your values and time availability.

Context 4: Personal Growth and Self-Development

Living by your principles also means applying them to your journey of personal growth. This involves setting goals that are aligned with your core values and seeking opportunities to stretch and challenge yourself. If your principle is "continuous learning," this might look like committing to a daily reading habit, attending workshops, or even engaging in conversations with people who have different perspectives to broaden your understanding.

When I embraced the principle of "humility in learning," I sought out mentors and courses that pushed me out of my comfort zone. I deliberately chose learning environments where I wasn't the most knowledgeable person in the room, which kept me grounded and constantly learning. This approach has not only expanded my skills but also deepened my appreciation for lifelong growth.

Key Takeaway: Principles that support personal growth, like humility and curiosity, can transform challenges into learning opportunities.

Potential Challenge: Fear of stepping outside your comfort zone. **Solution:** Start with small, manageable steps and gradually build your confidence by taking on bigger challenges.

Context 5: Navigating Challenges and Adversity

Applying your principles during times of adversity is perhaps the most challenging but also the most rewarding. It's easy to live by your values when things are going smoothly, but the true test comes when life gets tough.

If "resilience" is one of your principles, it might mean choosing to stay committed to your goals even when you face setbacks or approaching failure as a learning opportunity rather than a reason to quit.

During a particularly tough period in my career, where nothing seemed to be going right, I held onto my principle of "perseverance through adversity." Instead of giving up, I doubled down on my efforts, reached out for support, and sought ways to learn from the setbacks. That challenging period taught me more about resilience than any easy victory ever could.

Key Takeaway: Adversity is an opportunity to strengthen and reaffirm your principles, building character and resilience.

Potential Challenge: Feeling overwhelmed by setbacks and losing motivation. **Solution:** Break down challenges into smaller steps, seek support from your network, and focus on progress rather than perfection.

Context 6: Leadership and Influence

In leadership roles, whether in your professional life, family, or community, applying your principles is crucial for building trust and fostering a positive environment. If one of your principles is "lead by example," this might mean demonstrating the behavior you expect from others, being transparent about your decisions, and showing vulnerability when necessary.

As a leader in my organization, I made it a point to practice "lead by example." When we faced a crisis, I was upfront about the challenges and invited my team to collaborate on solutions. This openness not only reinforced trust but also empowered others to take ownership of their roles.

Key Takeaway: Principles like transparency and empathy in leadership create a culture of trust and collaboration.

Potential Challenge: Balancing transparency with the need for discretion. **Solution:** Share openly within appropriate boundaries, focusing on solutions rather than problems.

Context 7: Financial Decision-Making

Applying principles in financial contexts can help guide decisions around spending, investing, and managing resources. If "responsibility" is a core principle, this might mean being intentional about your financial choices, such as creating a budget, saving for the future, and avoiding impulsive purchases.

For example, my principle of "financial stewardship" guides me to make thoughtful investments that align with my long-term goals and values. I regularly assess my financial decisions to ensure they support not only my personal growth but also my ability to give back to my community.

Key Takeaway: Principles like responsibility and stewardship help create a balanced and value-aligned financial life.

Potential Challenge: Balancing financial discipline with enjoying life. **Solution:** Create a balanced budget that allows for both responsible saving and enjoyable spending.

Context 8: Health and Well-being

Your principles can also guide decisions about your health and well-being. If "self-care" is one of your core values, this might mean prioritizing regular exercise, a balanced diet, adequate rest, and mindfulness practices. It's about making choices that honor your body and mind.

When I adopted the principle of "self-care as a priority," I committed to regular exercise and mindful eating. This was not just about physical health but also about honoring my body as a vessel for living out my mission.

Key Takeaway: Health-related principles support a balanced lifestyle that empowers you to live your values fully.

Potential Challenge: Staying committed to health goals amidst a busy schedule. **Solution:** Plan and prepare in advance, integrating self-care into your daily routine.

Context 9: Parenting and Family Life

Applying principles in parenting and family life can shape the environment and values that you pass down to future generations. If one of your principles is "teaching through example," it means modeling the behaviors and values you want your children to learn, such as kindness, responsibility, and resilience.

I often remind myself of the principle of "lead with love" when interacting with my children. This principle guides me to prioritize understanding, patience, and encouragement in every situation, even when discipline is needed.

Key Takeaway: Principles applied in parenting foster a positive and values-driven environment for growth.

Potential Challenge: Balancing discipline with empathy.
Solution: Use empathetic communication techniques and explain the values behind your decisions.

Context 10: Conflict Resolution

Principles are especially crucial when resolving conflicts, whether in personal or professional settings. If one of your core principles is "seek understanding," this might mean approaching conflicts with a willingness to listen and find common ground rather than jumping to conclusions or defending your position.

In a workplace conflict, I once applied the principle of "seek understanding before being understood." This approach helped defuse tension and opened the door to a more collaborative solution that benefited everyone involved.

Key Takeaway: Principles like empathy and understanding can turn conflicts into opportunities for growth and connection.

Potential Challenge: Managing emotions during conflicts.
Solution: Practice active listening, take a moment to breathe, and approach the situation with an open mind.

Your Homework

Identify three areas of your life—career, relationships, community, personal growth, challenges, leadership, finance, health, parenting, or conflict—where you feel you could better apply your principles. For each area, write down one specific action you will take this week to live more authentically according to your values.

PRO TIP: Remember that applying your principles is a practice, not a one-time effort. Start with small, intentional actions and build from there. Over time, you'll find that living by your values becomes second nature, no matter the context.

By applying your principles in different life contexts, you turn them into more than just words; you turn them into a way of life. Each context offers a unique opportunity to live more fully and authentically, deepening your commitment to your true self.

Quotables from this Section

> *"Your principles are your guiding light; apply them consistently across all areas of life."*

> *"Living by your values in different contexts deepens your commitment to them."*

> *"Principles are not just ideas; they are actions that shape your reality."*

DISCUSSION QUESTIONS

1. Discuss how you apply your core principles in different areas of your life, such as work, family, and community.

2. How do you ensure consistency in living by your values across various life contexts?

3. Reflect on a time when applying your principles in a different context led to unexpected growth or insights.

NORMALIZE THE MISSION

"What you do every day matters more than what you do once in a while." — Gretchen Rubin

Once you've defined your principles and committed them to memory, the next step is to weave them seamlessly into the fabric of your daily life.

This is where you normalize your mission—transforming your principles from lofty ideals into everyday actions that define how you live, work, and interact with others.

Normalizing your mission means making these principles an automatic part of your mindset and behaviors so they guide you without conscious effort.

Step 1: Integrate Your Principles into Daily Habits

To normalize your mission, start by integrating your principles into your daily habits and routines. Look for specific moments in your day where you can practice your values.

For example, if one of your principles is "active listening," make it a habit to put away distractions and be fully present during every conversation, whether at work or at home. If "service to others" is a core value, consider ways to incorporate small acts of kindness or support into your daily interactions.

One way I do this is by starting each day with a short reflection on how I can embody my principles. For instance, I ask myself: *How can I lead with integrity today? How can I show humility in my interactions?* These questions set the tone for the day and make my principles actionable and practical.

Transition to Next Step: Normalizing your mission isn't just about what you do alone; it's also about the systems and structures that support these actions.

Step 2: Create Systems that Reinforce Your Mission

Building systems around your principles can help reinforce them until they become second nature. For example, if your principle is "growth through learning," set up a system where you dedicate 30 minutes each day to reading, listening to a podcast, or taking an online course.

Make it a routine and block it out on your calendar as an appointment with yourself. Systems provide structure and consistency, making it easier to live by your principles without having to constantly think about it.

I've built a system around continuous learning by scheduling a "power hour" every morning where I dive into a book, podcast, or reflective journaling. This system not only reinforces my principle of growth but also sets a productive tone for the day.

Key Takeaway: By creating systems, you reduce the mental load required to live by your principles, allowing them to become more ingrained in your daily actions.

Potential Challenge: You may struggle to keep up with new systems initially. **Solution:** Start small—integrate one principle into your routine at a time and gradually build from there.

Step 3: Surround Yourself with Supportive People

Who you surround yourself with significantly impacts whether you normalize your mission or not. Seek out people who embody similar values or who encourage and support your growth. These individuals will not only help keep you accountable but also provide a positive environment that reinforces your mission. Consider joining communities, mastermind groups, or networks that align with your principles and push you to live them out fully.

In my life, I've found it invaluable to stay connected with mentors, fellow coaches, and friends who challenge me to live by my principles. We often share our weekly wins and challenges, and having these discussions keeps me grounded and focused on my mission.

Key Takeaway: The company you keep can either reinforce or undermine your commitment to your principles. Choose wisely.

Potential Challenge: Not everyone will understand or support your mission. **Solution:** Politely distance yourself from negative influences and seek out new relationships that better align with your values.

Step 4: Use Reminders and Rituals to Stay Grounded

Create reminders and rituals that help you stay connected to your mission. These could be as simple as a morning meditation that focuses on your principles, setting alarms throughout the day with affirmations, or having a weekly family or team meeting where you reflect on how well everyone lived out the agreed-upon values. Rituals help reinforce what matters most, making your mission feel natural and ingrained in your daily rhythm.

For example, in my coaching work, we would start each practice or meeting with a grounding ritual that reminded everyone of our shared values and goals. This small but intentional practice helped normalize the mission for the team and created a culture where those principles were lived out daily.

Key Takeaway: Rituals anchor your principles in daily actions, making them harder to forget and easier to live by.

Potential Challenge: Rituals can feel monotonous over time. **Solution:** Periodically refresh your rituals to keep them meaningful and engaging.

Step 5: Reflect and Adjust Regularly

Normalizing your mission is not a one-time event; it's an ongoing process.

Regularly reflect on how well you're living by your principles and whether your mission still aligns with your current goals and values. Set aside time weekly or monthly to assess how your principles are influencing your decisions and actions. Are there areas where you're falling short? Are there any adjustments needed? Reflection keeps your mission dynamic and relevant.

I conduct a "mission check" every month, where I review my actions and decisions against my principles. It's a chance to celebrate where I'm on track and course-correct where I'm not. This practice has been crucial in ensuring my mission remains aligned with my evolving goals and life circumstances.

Key Takeaway: Regular reflection prevents stagnation and ensures your mission remains aligned with who you are becoming.

Potential Challenge: It can be easy to forget to reflect amidst a busy life. **Solution:** Schedule your reflection times and treat them as non-negotiable appointments.

Step 6: Teach and Model Your Mission

One of the most powerful ways to normalize your mission is to teach it to others. Whether it's within your family, team, or community, sharing your principles and modeling them consistently reinforces them not just for yourself, but for those around you. Teaching creates a higher level of accountability and makes your mission a living, breathing part of your daily interactions.

When I was coaching young athletes, I often shared stories of how our team principles—like resilience and integrity—played out in real-life scenarios. By modeling these principles and discussing them openly, the mission became a shared standard that everyone aspired to.

Key Takeaway: Teaching your principles to others reinforces your commitment to them and helps build a community aligned with your values.

Potential Challenge: Teaching requires vulnerability and consistency. **Solution:** Start small, share your principles in safe environments, and build from there.

Your Homework

Identify three daily habits or routines where you can integrate your principles more fully. Create one system that reinforces a core value and commit to it for the next 30 days. Surround yourself with at least two people who share or support your mission, and schedule a regular time for reflection and adjustment.

PRO TIP: Remember, normalizing your mission is about consistency, not perfection. It's better to focus on small, sustainable changes than to aim for drastic transformations that are hard to maintain.

By normalizing your mission, you transform your principles from abstract ideas into a way of life. You create a foundation that supports you in being your authentic self, every day, in every interaction.

QUOTABLES FROM THIS SECTION

> *"Success is built on daily habits, not occasional bursts of effort."*
>
> *"Make your mission a natural part of your daily routine; consistency is key."*
>
> *"Surround yourself with an environment that supports and reflects your values."*

Discussion questions

1. What daily habits or routines have you found effective in keeping you aligned with your mission?

2. How can you create an environment that naturally supports living by your principles?

3. Discuss the importance of making your mission a natural part of your everyday life. How do you achieve this balance?

DEVELOPING A PERSONAL GROWTH PLAN

"The best way to predict the future is to create it." — Peter Drucker

Living by your principles requires more than just good intentions; it requires a well-thought-out plan that guides your actions, keeps you focused, and helps you measure your progress.

A personal growth plan is like a roadmap that lays out the steps you need to take to become the person you aspire to be. It's a practical tool that aligns your daily actions with your long-term goals, ensuring that you stay on course and make continuous progress.

Step 1: Set Clear, Principle-Based Goals

Start by setting specific, principle-based goals that are aligned with your core values. Your goals should reflect who you want to become, not just what you want to achieve.

For instance, if one of your principles is "continuous learning," a goal might be to read one new book each month or take a course that challenges your thinking. Make your goals clear, measurable, and connected to your principles. Ask yourself: *How does this goal reflect my core values? What impact will achieving this goal have on my growth journey?*

For example, my principle of "servant leadership" led me to set a goal of mentoring three young coaches each year. This goal not only aligns with my values but also reinforces my commitment to giving back and fostering growth in others.

Step 2: Break Down Goals into Manageable Steps

Big goals can be daunting, which is why breaking them down into smaller, manageable steps is crucial. Identify the specific actions you need to take to move toward each goal. These could be daily, weekly, or monthly tasks that keep you progressing steadily. Breaking down your goals helps create a clear path forward and prevents you from feeling overwhelmed.

For instance, if your goal is to improve public speaking, start with smaller steps like joining a local speaking club, practicing weekly in front of a mirror, or seeking feedback from a trusted friend. These smaller actions build confidence and momentum toward your larger goal.

Step 3: Create a Timeline and Track Your Progress

A goal without a timeline is just a wish. Establish a realistic timeframe for each goal and its associated steps. This timeline should motivate you to stay on track without causing undue stress. Consider using a planner, digital calendar, or growth journal to map out your timeline and track your progress. Regularly review and adjust your timeline as needed to accommodate changes in your life or priorities.

I use a simple spreadsheet to track my progress on different growth goals. This allows me to see where I'm on track and where I need to refocus my efforts. It's a small but effective tool that keeps me accountable and committed to my growth journey.

Step 4: Build in Reflection and Adjustment Periods

Reflection is a key component of any growth plan. Set aside time every month or quarter to reflect on your progress. Ask yourself: *What have I achieved so far? Where have I faced challenges? How have my experiences shaped or refined my principles?*

Reflection allows you to assess whether your goals are still aligned with your values and if any adjustments are needed. Growth is not a straight line, and being flexible and adaptive is essential for staying on course.

Every three months, I hold a personal "growth review" where I assess my progress, celebrate wins, and make adjustments to my goals. This practice helps me stay aligned with my principles while remaining open to new opportunities for growth.

Step 5: Use Tools and Resources to Support Your Plan

Utilize tools and resources that can help you stay organized and motivated. This could include growth journals, habit trackers, digital apps, or accountability groups. Identify what works best for you and commit to using those tools regularly.

They serve as both reminders and motivators to keep you moving forward.

For instance, I use a combination of a digital planner for daily tasks and a physical journal for deeper reflection and note-taking. These tools complement each other and provide a balanced approach to managing both my short-term actions and long-term growth.

Step 6: Celebrate Milestones and Adjust for New Goals

As you achieve your goals, take time to celebrate those milestones. Acknowledging your progress is important for maintaining motivation and reinforcing positive behavior. Each milestone is a testament to your commitment to your principles. However, growth is a continuous journey. As you reach one goal, be ready to set new ones that align with your evolving understanding of yourself.

When I reached my goal of completing an advanced coaching certification, I took a moment to celebrate that achievement. But I also recognized it as a stepping stone, prompting me to set a new goal to train and mentor upcoming coaches using what I had learned.

Your Homework: Take time this week to draft a personal growth plan. Identify three principle-based goals you want to achieve in the next six months. Break down each goal into manageable steps, create a timeline, and choose tools that will help you track your progress. Schedule a reflection period in your calendar and commit to adjusting your plan as needed.

PRO TIP: Keep your growth plan dynamic. Life changes, and so should your plan. Revisit it regularly, stay flexible, and be willing to adapt your goals to reflect your ongoing growth and evolving values.

By developing a personal growth plan, you create a structured path to living out your principles and achieving meaningful progress. It's more than a set of goals—it's a commitment to becoming the best version of yourself, one step at a time.

Quotables from this Section

> *"The best growth plans are intentional, flexible, and aligned with your values."*

> *"Plan for the future you want by creating it today."*

> *"Your growth is a lifelong journey; be willing to adapt and evolve."*

Discussion Questions

1. What steps do you take to develop and maintain a personal growth plan?

2. How can you ensure that your growth plan aligns with your core values and principles?

3. Discuss the importance of flexibility in a growth plan. How do you adapt when things don't go as planned?

REVISIT AND EVOLVE YOUR PRINCIPLES OVER TIME

"Change is the law of life. And those who look only to the past or present are certain to miss the future." — John F. Kennedy

Life is dynamic, and so are you. As you grow and encounter new experiences, your understanding of your principles may deepen, and new values may emerge. Just as seasons change, so too might your priorities, perspectives, and goals.

Reassessing and evolving your principles is not a sign of inconsistency but rather of growth and self-awareness. This process allows your principles to remain aligned with who you are becoming.

Step 1: Schedule Regular "Principle Check-Ups"

Just as you might schedule a physical check-up or a performance review, it's essential to schedule regular "principle check-ups" to reflect on how your values are serving you.

These check-ups can be quarterly, semi-annually, or annually, depending on what feels right for you. During these sessions, ask yourself: *Are my principles still aligned with my current goals and values? Have recent experiences changed my perspective on any of my core beliefs?*

For example, after a major career change, I took time to reassess my principles. I realized that "innovation" needed to be more prominent in my values, as my new role required a more forward-thinking mindset. This reflection helped me adjust and better align my principles with my new professional path.

Key Takeaway: Regularly revisiting your principles ensures they remain relevant and reflective of your evolving self.

Potential Challenge: Forgetting to schedule or prioritize these reflections. **Solution:** Set a recurring reminder on your calendar and treat it as a non-negotiable appointment.

Step 2: Reflect on Major Life Events and Transitions

Significant life events—such as a new job, a move, a loss, or a personal breakthrough—often lead to a shift in perspective. Use these moments as opportunities to revisit your principles. Reflect on what these events have taught you and how they have impacted your core values. Have your priorities shifted? Has your understanding of a particular principle deepened?

When I became a parent, my principle of "lead with empathy" took on a new dimension. I realized empathy wasn't just about understanding others but also about being patient with myself and allowing room for growth as I navigated new challenges. This shift led me to refine my principles to include self-compassion as a key value.

Key Takeaway: Major life changes provide fertile ground for reassessing and evolving your principles to better serve your new reality.

Potential Challenge: Feeling overwhelmed by change and not knowing how to adapt your principles. **Solution:** Start with small adjustments and allow your principles to evolve naturally over time.

Step 3: Use a Principle Evolution Worksheet

A structured approach can help make the process of revisiting and evolving your principles more manageable. Consider using a "Principle Evolution Worksheet" that includes prompts such as:

- What experiences over the past 6-12 months have challenged my principles?

- Are there new values that have emerged from these experiences?

- Which principles feel most relevant now, and why?

- Are there any principles that no longer serve me or need to be reframed?

By working through these questions, you can gain clarity on where your principles stand and where they may need to evolve.

Key Takeaway: A structured worksheet provides clarity and direction when revisiting your principles, ensuring they remain impactful and meaningful.

Potential Challenge: Not knowing where to start with revising your principles. **Solution:** Focus on one principle at a time, using the worksheet to guide your thought process.

Step 4: Embrace Flexibility Without Losing Core Values

While it's important to be open to change, it's equally crucial to ensure that your evolving principles remain true to your core values. Flexibility means adapting your principles to fit your current reality, not abandoning what's most important. Ask yourself: *Is this new principle a reflection of my authentic self, or is it a reaction to external pressures?* This reflection helps ensure that any changes are made for the right reasons.

For example, after facing burnout from overcommitment, I realized that my principle of "service to others" needed to be balanced with "service to self." This wasn't about abandoning service but rather recognizing that self-care was essential to continue serving others effectively.

Key Takeaway: Evolving your principles doesn't mean losing your core values; it's about finding balance and authenticity in their application.

Potential Challenge: Confusing flexibility with inconsistency. **Solution:** Keep your core values at the heart of any adjustments and ensure they align with your true self.

Step 5: Seek Feedback and Insights from Trusted Sources

Sometimes, we need an outside perspective to help us see clearly. Share your evolving principles with trusted friends, mentors, or colleagues who understand your journey and values. Ask for their insights on whether your revised principles resonate and reflect who you are becoming. Their feedback can provide valuable confirmation or encourage you to dig deeper.

I once sought feedback from a mentor when I was considering adjusting my principles to include "creative risk-taking." Her insights helped me recognize that while this principle was important, I also needed to define what "calculated risk" meant to me to avoid impulsivity. This refinement made my principle clearer and more actionable.

Key Takeaway: Feedback from trusted sources helps validate your evolving principles and provides a fresh perspective on your growth journey.

Potential Challenge: Fear of being judged or criticized for changing your principles. **Solution:** Choose individuals who support your growth and approach feedback with an open mind.

Step 6: Document the Evolution of Your Principles

Keep a journal or digital document that tracks the evolution of your principles over time. Note the changes you make, the reasons behind them, and the experiences that led to these adjustments. This documentation not only serves as a reflective tool but also provides a sense of continuity and progress in your growth journey.

When I look back at my principle journal, I see how my values have evolved from my early 20s to now. This reflection helps me appreciate my growth and better understand how past experiences have shaped who I am today.

Key Takeaway: Documenting your principle evolution allows you to see your growth journey more clearly and appreciate the progress you've made.

Potential Challenge: Not keeping up with documentation. **Solution:** Set aside time once a month to update your principle evolution journal.

Step 7: Recommit to Your Evolved Principles

After revising and refining your principles, recommit to them with renewed clarity and purpose. Treat them as a living document that will continue to guide your actions and decisions. Consider creating a new ritual, such as a monthly affirmation or a symbolic act, to reinforce your commitment to these evolved principles.

For example, after refining my principles, I created a ritual where I read them aloud every first day of the month and set a specific intention for how I will embody them in the coming weeks. This practice keeps my principles fresh and top of mind.

Key Takeaway: Recommitting to your evolved principles ensures they continue to guide you with renewed energy and focus.

Potential Challenge: Feeling disconnected from new principles. **Solution:** Give yourself time to adjust and create rituals that reinforce their importance.

Your Homework

Set a date for your next "principle check-up" and use the Principle Evolution Worksheet to reflect on your values and their relevance to your current life. Share your revised principles with a trusted friend or mentor and ask for feedback. Document any changes and create a ritual to recommit to your principles.

PRO TIP: Remember, the evolution of your principles is a natural part of growth. Embrace it as a sign of self-awareness and adaptability, and let your principles grow with you.

By regularly revisiting and evolving your principles, you ensure they remain aligned with who you are and who you aspire to become. This ongoing process of reflection and adjustment allows you to live more authentically, embracing growth and change as natural parts of the journey.

QUOTABLES FROM THIS SECTION

> *"Principles are not set in stone; they should grow as you grow."*

> *"Revisiting your principles keeps them relevant and impactful."*

> *"Embrace change; it is the law of life and the key to growth."*

DISCUSSION QUESTIONS

1. How do you know when it's time to revisit and evolve your principles?

   _____
   _____
   _____
   _____

2. Discuss a time when you had to adjust your values or beliefs based on new experiences or insights.

   _____
   _____
   _____
   _____

3. How can embracing change help you stay aligned with your true self over time?

   _____
   _____
   _____
   _____

CONCLUSION

There is NO substitute for peace of mind, no go and live it.

As you come to the end of this journey, remember that the work of understanding yourself, defining your principles, and living by them is never truly finished. It is an ongoing process—a dynamic journey of growth, reflection, and adaptation.

Each step you've taken in this book, from self-reflection to extracting life principles, committing to memory, and normalizing your mission, is about aligning more closely with who you are meant to be.

Revisit Your Foundation Often

Your principles are the foundation upon which you build your life. They guide your actions, shape your decisions, and influence the way you interact with the world. But like any foundation, they require maintenance. Revisit them regularly. Reflect on your experiences and adjust your principles as needed.

Life is not static, and neither should your values be. Ask yourself: *Does this principle still resonate with who I am today? How has my understanding of it evolved through new experiences?*

Make it a habit to engage in this reflection at the start of each new season or year. This practice will keep you grounded in your core values while allowing you to grow and adapt as needed.

Embrace the Power of Your Story

Your story—your experiences, heritage, challenges, and triumphs—is uniquely yours. It is a wellspring of wisdom and strength that no one else possesses. Embrace it fully.

Use it as a guide to navigate life's challenges and as a source of inspiration to keep pushing forward. Remember that your journey is not just about finding success, but about becoming the person you were always meant to be. You are both the author and the hero of your story. Write it boldly, live it authentically, and share it generously.

Consider sharing your story and principles with a mentor, a close friend, or a community. There's immense power in expressing your mission and inviting others to hold you accountable.

For me, embracing my story meant leaning into my roots and using the values instilled in me by my family, culture, and experiences to shape my path. It's about recognizing that each setback is an opportunity to learn, each success a moment to reflect on what truly matters, and each day a chance to live more fully in alignment with my principles.

Continue to Seek Growth and Authenticity

Living a life of purpose and authenticity is not about achieving a perfect state of being. It's about the willingness to continuously grow, adapt, and evolve. Embrace the discomfort that comes with growth. Seek out experiences that challenge you and push you beyond your comfort zone.

Be open to new perspectives and be willing to unlearn what no longer serves you. Authenticity requires courage—the courage to stand firm in your values even when it's difficult and the courage to evolve those values when needed.

Take time every few months to ask yourself: *What new experiences or learnings have shaped me recently? How can I refine my principles to reflect my evolving understanding of myself?*

Inspire Others by Living Your Mission

As you live out your principles and normalize your mission, you naturally inspire others around you. Your actions, consistency, and authenticity can create a ripple effect that encourages others to embark on their own journey of self-discovery and growth.

Whether you're leading a team, raising a family, or building a community, remember that your commitment to living authentically will resonate far beyond what you can see. By embodying your principles, you become a living example of what it means to live a life of integrity and purpose.

I've seen this in my own life as a coach, mentor, and leader. When I stayed true to my principles, even in challenging times, it inspired those around me to do the same. It reminded me that our greatest impact often comes not from what we say, but from how we choose to live.

Your Journey is Just Beginning

While this book may be ending, your journey is just beginning. Take what you've learned, and make it your own. Continue to explore, reflect, and refine. Trust in the process and trust in yourself. The road ahead will have its share of obstacles, but with your principles as your guide, you have the tools to navigate whatever comes your way.

Visualize where you see yourself in a year if you live by your principles every day. What does that future look like? What steps can you take today to move closer to that vision? The road ahead is yours to shape.

Remember that every step forward is progress, every lesson learned is valuable, and every moment is an opportunity to grow. Keep moving with intention, stay rooted in your values, and never stop becoming the best version of yourself.

Thank you for allowing me to share this journey with you. May you walk forward with clarity, courage, and purpose, and may you always stay true to the mission you've set for your life.

Final Thought: *Your life is a canvas, and your principles are the brushstrokes. Paint it with purpose, color it with authenticity, and let it be a masterpiece that reflects the essence of who you are. Share it with the world, and let your journey inspire others to find their own.*

SPECIAL BONUS SECTIONS

The three new special bonus sections—**Mindset Shifts**, **Illustrative Analogies**, and **Biblical Encouragement**—are designed to provide readers with deeper insights, practical applications, and spiritual inspiration to enhance their personal growth journey.

These sections add value by offering diverse approaches to understanding and internalizing the core messages of the book, making the content more relatable, actionable, and memorable.

Mindset Shifts

The "Mindset Shifts" section is designed to encourage readers to rethink their existing beliefs and perspectives in a way that aligns with the core themes of each chapter.

By introducing new ways of thinking, this section helps readers break free from limiting mindsets and adopt more empowering and growth-oriented views. Each mindset shift is presented with a description, an explanation of how it relates to the chapter's content, and a reflective prompt to help readers internalize the shift.

This approach ensures that readers not only understand the concept intellectually but also apply it practically to their own lives.

How Readers Can Use This Section:

1. **Challenge Existing Beliefs**: Each mindset shift encourages readers to question their current ways of thinking and to consider more constructive and growth-oriented alternatives. By reflecting on these shifts, readers can identify limiting beliefs that may be holding them back and begin to replace them with more empowering perspectives.

2. **Deepen Personal Reflection**: The reflective prompts provided for each mindset shift serve as powerful tools for introspection. Readers can use these prompts as journaling exercises to explore their thoughts and

emotions more deeply, leading to greater self-awareness and personal growth. For example, a prompt might ask, "Where in your life are you trying to please others rather than staying true to yourself?" This can help readers uncover areas where they may need to make changes to live more authentically.

3. **Apply New Perspectives in Real Life**: The mindset shifts are designed to be practical and applicable to everyday situations. Readers can take the insights gained from each shift and apply them immediately to their relationships, careers, personal growth, and other areas of life. By consciously adopting these new mindsets, they can navigate challenges more effectively and make decisions that align with their values.

4. **Facilitate Group Discussion and Learning**: In a group setting, such as a book club or study group, these mindset shifts can serve as excellent discussion starters. Each shift presents an opportunity to share personal experiences, insights, and strategies for growth. Group members can discuss how adopting a particular mindset could help them overcome specific challenges or achieve their goals.

5. **Encourage Continuous Growth**: This section helps readers understand that personal growth is not a one-time event but an ongoing process of evolving and adapting. By revisiting the mindset shifts regularly, readers can reinforce their commitment to personal development and remain open to new ways of thinking and being.

6. **Integrate with Other Sections**: The mindset shifts complement other elements of the book, such as reflection prompts, journaling exercises, and action steps. Readers can use the shifts alongside these other tools to create a comprehensive personal development plan that includes both internal mindset work and external action.

Using This Section Effectively:

- **Personal Journaling**: Readers can set aside time each week to reflect on one mindset shift and its corresponding prompt, journaling about how it applies to their current life situation and what changes they can make.

- **Mentoring and Coaching**: These mindset shifts can also be valuable for mentors and coaches who are helping others navigate their personal growth journeys. They can use the shifts to guide conversations, offer new perspectives, and encourage deeper reflection.

- **Habit Formation**: By choosing a mindset shift to focus on for a month, readers can actively work to integrate that new perspective into their daily habits and routines, reinforcing positive change over time.

The "Mindset Shifts" section is a powerful resource for anyone looking to grow, transform, and live more intentionally. It invites readers to embark on a journey of continuous self-discovery and evolution, equipping them with the tools needed to thrive in all areas of life.

1. Introduction

- **Mindset Shift**: From Seeking Validation to Embracing Authenticity

- **Description**: Focus on being authentic to yourself rather than seeking external approval. True fulfillment comes from living in alignment with your own values.

- **How It Relates to the Section**: The introduction discusses the importance of being "rooted in culture" and staying true to one's values. This mindset shift aligns with the core message of grounding oneself in internal values rather than external validation.

- **Prompt for Reflection**: Where in your life are you trying to please others rather than staying true to yourself?

2. Hi, I'm Rob Pene

- **Mindset Shift**: From Fear of the Unknown to Curiosity for Growth

- **Description**: View unfamiliar situations as opportunities for learning rather than threats. Embrace uncertainty with curiosity and see it as a chance to grow.

- **How It Relates to the Section**: This section introduces Rob's story and how he navigated different environments and cultures. The mindset shift emphasizes the growth that comes from embracing new and uncomfortable situations.

- **Prompt for Reflection**: How can approaching a current challenge with curiosity change your outlook?

3. From American Samoa

- **Mindset Shift**: From Viewing Heritage as a Limitation to Seeing It as a Strength

- **Description**: Recognize that your cultural heritage provides a solid foundation for growth, offering wisdom, resilience, and a unique perspective.

- **How It Relates to the Section**: This section talks about the cultural values of American Samoa and how they shape one's identity. The mindset shift encourages readers to see their heritage as a strength that contributes to their resilience and character.

- **Prompt for Reflection**: How can you use your cultural background as a source of strength?

4. Tony Solaita Little League

- **Mindset Shift**: From Seeing Adversity as a Setback to Viewing It as a Teacher

- **Description**: Challenges are not roadblocks but essential lessons that build character, resilience, and a warrior spirit.

- **How It Relates to the Section**: This section discusses the life lessons learned on the baseball field, which parallel the idea that every hardship is a chance to learn and grow stronger.

- **Prompt for Reflection**: Think of a recent challenge. What lesson did it teach you?

5. Importance of Cultural Heritage

- **Mindset Shift**: From Ignoring the Past to Drawing Strength from It

- **Description**: Instead of disregarding the past, see it as a source of strength, wisdom, and guidance that can help you face the present and future.

- **How It Relates to the Section**: This section emphasizes the value of understanding and embracing one's cultural heritage to make better decisions and live authentically.

- **Prompt for Reflection**: How has understanding your cultural heritage helped you make better decisions?

6. Extracting Life Principles

- **Mindset Shift**: From Letting Life Happen to Defining Your Path

- **Description**: Instead of drifting through life, take active steps to define your core principles that will guide your decisions and actions.

- **How It Relates to the Section**: This section encourages readers to be intentional about their values and principles, much like setting a compass for one's life journey.

- **Prompt for Reflection**: What are three principles that currently guide your life? Are they serving you well?

7. Be a Student of Yourself

- **Mindset Shift**: From Self-Judgment to Self-Discovery

- **Description**: Move away from harsh self-criticism and towards a mindset of curiosity and learning about who you are.

- **How It Relates to the Section**: This section focuses on the importance of continuous self-reflection and growth. The mindset shift encourages a compassionate approach to self-study.

- **Prompt for Reflection**: What is one thing you've learned about yourself recently? How can this insight help you grow?

8. Interview Others About You

- **Mindset Shift**: From Assuming You Know Yourself to Valuing Outside Perspectives

- **Description**: Recognize that others' perceptions can provide valuable insights into who you are and how you're seen in the world.

- **How It Relates to the Section**: This section suggests seeking feedback from others to understand oneself better, highlighting the importance of outside perspectives.

- **Prompt for Reflection**: What's the most surprising feedback you've received about yourself? How did it impact you?

9. Organize the Data

- **Mindset Shift**: From Overwhelmed by Information to Empowered by Clarity

- **Description**: Instead of being paralyzed by too much information, learn to organize your insights to gain clarity and direction.

- **How It Relates to the Section**: This section talks about gathering data from self-reflection and interviews and then organizing it to create actionable insights.

- **Prompt for Reflection**: What's one way you can better organize your thoughts or plans to gain more clarity?

10. Create a Manifesto

- **Mindset Shift**: From Wandering Aimlessly to Declaring Your Purpose

- **Description**: Shift from living reactively to living proactively by clearly defining what you stand for and what you strive to achieve.

- **How It Relates to the Section**: This section emphasizes creating a personal manifesto as a guiding document for one's life, reflecting core values and purpose.

- **Prompt for Reflection**: What would the first line of your personal manifesto be?

11. Overcoming Setbacks

- **Mindset Shift**: From Fearing Failure to Embracing Growth Opportunities

- **Description**: View failures not as dead ends but as valuable opportunities for growth and resilience.

- **How It Relates to the Section**: This section encourages seeing setbacks as opportunities for growth rather than obstacles to success.

- **Prompt for Reflection**: How can you reframe a recent setback as a learning opportunity?

12. Commit to Memory and Practice

- **Mindset Shift**: From Knowing to Doing

- **Description**: Move beyond merely knowing your principles to actively practicing them every day.

- **How It Relates to the Section**: This section stresses the importance of not just knowing your values but also committing them to memory and practice.

- **Prompt for Reflection**: What is one principle you know but struggle to practice? What step can you take today to start living it?

13. Building a Support System

- **Mindset Shift**: From Going It Alone to Building a Community

- **Description**: Recognize the power of a strong support system and actively seek out relationships that uplift and challenge you.

- **How It Relates to the Section**: This section discusses the importance of surrounding yourself with people who help you grow and hold you accountable.

- **Prompt for Reflection**: Who are the people that currently make up your support system? How do they help you grow?

14. Applying Principles in Different Life Contexts

- **Mindset Shift**: From Compartmentalizing Your Values to Living Consistently

- **Description**: Instead of having different values for different situations, aim to live by the same principles across all areas of life.

- **How It Relates to the Section**: This section discusses applying your principles consistently, regardless of context, to maintain authenticity and integrity.

- **Prompt for Reflection**: Are there areas of your life where you struggle to apply your core principles? How can you bring more consistency?

15. Normalize the Mission

- **Mindset Shift**: From Occasional Efforts to Daily Commitments

- **Description**: Make your mission a part of your everyday routine rather than something you pursue only occasionally.

- **How It Relates to the Section**: This section focuses on integrating your mission into daily habits and routines to ensure long-term commitment.

- **Prompt for Reflection**: What daily habit can you start to help normalize your mission in your life?

16. Developing a Personal Growth Plan

- **Mindset Shift**: From Wishing for Growth to Planning for It

- **Description**: Instead of hoping for personal growth, create a structured plan that outlines steps and milestones to achieve it.

- **How It Relates to the Section**: This section emphasizes the importance of having a personal growth plan that is intentional, flexible, and aligned with your values.

- **Prompt for Reflection**: What's one area of your life where you need a more concrete growth plan?

17. Revisit and Evolve Your Principles Over Time

- **Mindset Shift**: From Stagnation to Continuous Evolution

- **Description**: Understand that growth requires revisiting and evolving your principles to stay aligned with your true self.

- **How It Relates to the Section**: This section encourages readers to regularly revisit and adjust their principles to ensure they remain relevant and impactful.

- **Prompt for Reflection**: How have your core principles changed over time, and what experiences prompted those changes?

These "Mindset Shifts" provide readers with actionable reflections and a fresh perspective on each chapter, helping them to think differently and apply the lessons in meaningful ways.

Illustrative Analogies

The "Illustrative Analogies" section serves as a creative tool to make the complex ideas and life lessons discussed in the book more accessible, relatable, and memorable for readers.

By comparing key concepts to universal experiences or natural phenomena, these analogies and metaphors help distill the essence of each chapter into simple, everyday terms.

This approach not only aids in comprehension but also deepens the reader's emotional and intellectual connection to the material.

How Readers Can Use This Section:

1. **Clarify Complex Concepts**: Analogies and metaphors break down complex ideas into familiar scenarios, making them easier to grasp and apply. Readers can use these comparisons to better understand how cultural principles or personal growth concepts relate to their own lives.

2. **Enhance Memory and Retention**: Just as stories are easier to remember than facts, analogies and metaphors create mental images that stick. Readers

can recall these vivid images when reflecting on the lessons in the book, ensuring that the key messages stay with them long after they've turned the last page.

3. **Facilitate Discussion and Reflection**: For group studies or book clubs, these analogies provide excellent starting points for discussion. Readers can share how they interpret the metaphors or discuss how the analogies relate to their own experiences, fostering deeper engagement and personal insight.

4. **Apply Lessons in Real Life**: The metaphors can serve as practical reminders in daily life. For example, remembering that "setbacks are like pruning a tree; it may seem like a loss, but it allows for new growth to flourish" can help someone see challenges as opportunities for growth rather than as failures.

5. **Encourage Creative Thinking**: Readers can be inspired to come up with their own analogies and metaphors that resonate with their unique perspectives and experiences. This practice encourages creative thinking and helps readers internalize the lessons in a way that is deeply personal to them.

Using This Section Effectively:

- **Journal Prompts**: After reading each analogy or metaphor, readers can reflect on how it applies to their current life situation. For instance, they might journal about how their own life principles serve as "the stars in the night sky" guiding them through darkness.

- **Group Activities**: Book clubs or study groups can use these analogies to create group exercises, like storytelling or role-playing, to explore each concept more deeply.

- **Personal Development Plans**: As readers develop their personal growth plans, they can incorporate these metaphors as reminders or motivators to keep them aligned with their goals.

This section is designed to be both a learning aid and a reflective tool, helping readers engage with the content in a meaningful and lasting way.

1. Introduction

- **Analogy**: "Your values are like the roots of a tree. Just as deep roots keep a tree steady during storms, strong values keep you grounded when life gets tough."

- **Metaphor**: "Navigating life without principles is like sailing a ship without a compass—you may move forward, but you'll never truly know where you're going."

2. Hi, I'm Rob Pene

- **Analogy**: "Understanding yourself is like peeling an onion; you must go layer by layer, sometimes shedding tears, to reach the core."

- **Metaphor**: "Life is a dance between the familiar and the unknown; learning the steps means embracing both comfort and challenge."

3. From American Samoa

- **Analogy**: "Culture is like a lighthouse on a foggy night; it helps us navigate our way home when we feel lost."

- **Metaphor**: "Our traditions are the threads that weave the fabric of our identity, connecting us to those who came before and those who will come after."

4. Tony Solaita Little League

- **Analogy**: "Life is like a baseball game—sometimes you hit home runs, and sometimes you strike out, but it's the effort and perseverance that define you."

- **Metaphor**: "Coaching under Tony was like being forged in a fire; it burned away the inessential and left only strength and resilience."

5. Importance of Cultural Heritage

- **Analogy**: "Your heritage is like a wellspring of wisdom; the deeper you draw, the more strength and clarity you gain."

- **Metaphor**: "Cultural heritage is the soil in which we grow; without rich, fertile ground, we cannot flourish."

6. Extracting Life Principles

- **Analogy**: "Extracting life principles is like mining for gold; it takes effort to dig deep, sift through the dirt, and find the precious nuggets that guide us."

- **Metaphor**: "Principles are the stars in the night sky of our lives; they guide us even when everything around us is dark."

7. Be a Student of Yourself

- **Analogy**: "Studying yourself is like gardening; you must tend to your growth, prune what no longer serves you, and nurture what does."

- **Metaphor**: "Self-reflection is a mirror that reveals not just who we are, but who we have the potential to become."

8. Interview Others About You

- **Analogy**: "Asking for feedback is like holding up multiple mirrors; each one reflects a different angle of who we are."

- **Metaphor**: "Feedback from others is the chisel that carves away our rough edges, helping us become the masterpiece we are meant to be."

9. Organize the Data

- **Analogy**: "Organizing your insights is like assembling a jigsaw puzzle; every piece is essential, but only when put together do you see the full picture."

- **Metaphor**: "Data without organization is like a river without banks; it flows everywhere but lacks direction and purpose."

10. Create a Manifesto

- **Analogy**: "A manifesto is like a lighthouse for your journey; it illuminates the way forward when the path is unclear."

- **Metaphor**: "Your manifesto is your personal constitution, a declaration of what you stand for and how you intend to live."

11. Overcoming Setbacks

- **Analogy**: "Setbacks are like pruning a tree; it may seem like a loss, but it allows for new growth to flourish."

- **Metaphor**: "Resilience is a rubber band; it stretches and bends but always returns to its original shape, stronger for having been tested."

12. Commit to Memory and Practice

- **Analogy**: "Committing to memory is like engraving words on stone; it makes your values permanent fixtures in your life."

- **Metaphor**: "Practice is the river that smooths the rough stones of our habits, turning them into polished gems over time."

13. Building a Support System

- **Analogy**: "A support system is like scaffolding on a building; it helps you rise higher than you could on your own."

- **Metaphor**: "The right people in your life are the wind beneath your wings, lifting you when you can't lift yourself."

14. Applying Principles in Different Life Contexts

- **Analogy**: "Applying principles across different contexts is like a chef using the same ingredients to create a variety of dishes; the core remains the same, but the outcomes are unique."

- **Metaphor**: "Principles are the roots, and life's various contexts are the branches; strong roots allow the branches to stretch wide and bear fruit."

15. Normalize the Mission

- **Analogy**: "Normalizing your mission is like planting seeds every day; small actions accumulate to create a thriving garden."

- **Metaphor**: "Consistency is the drumbeat that keeps the rhythm of your mission alive, even when the melody changes."

16. Developing a Personal Growth Plan

- **Analogy**: "A growth plan is like a blueprint for a house; without it, you're just stacking bricks without purpose."

- **Metaphor**: "Your growth plan is a roadmap; it doesn't guarantee a smooth journey, but it ensures you know where you're headed."

17. Revisit and Evolve Your Principles Over Time

- **Analogy**: "Revisiting your principles is like updating the software on your phone; it keeps everything running smoothly and aligned with the latest needs."

- **Metaphor**: "Principles are like rivers; they flow and change course with time but are always headed toward the ocean of truth."

These analogies and metaphors aim to simplify complex concepts and relate them to familiar experiences or natural phenomena, making them more accessible and memorable for readers.

Biblical Encouragement

The "Biblical Encouragement" section is designed to provide spiritual depth and guidance to the concepts presented in each chapter of the book.

By incorporating carefully chosen Bible verses, this section helps readers draw parallels between the teachings of scripture and the practical life lessons discussed throughout the book.

Each verse is accompanied by a brief description that explains its relevance to the section's theme, offering readers a holistic approach to understanding how faith, culture, and personal growth intersect.

How Readers Can Use This Section:

1. **Reflect and Meditate**: Readers are encouraged to reflect on the Bible verses and how they apply to their own lives. By meditating on these scriptures, they can find spiritual encouragement and wisdom that aligns with the lessons in the book. For instance, when reading about "Overcoming Setbacks," they can

meditate on James 1:2-3, which reminds them to view trials as opportunities for growth.

2. **Incorporate into Daily Devotions**: This section can be used as part of a daily devotional practice. Readers can focus on a specific verse that resonates with them and use it as a foundation for prayer, journaling, or group discussion. This allows them to explore how scripture can guide their journey toward personal development and cultural understanding.

3. **Enhance Group Discussions**: For book clubs or group studies, these Bible verses serve as powerful discussion starters. Groups can explore the relevance of each verse to the chapter's content and share personal reflections on how these scriptures have impacted their own lives. This shared exploration can foster deeper connections among members and enrich the study experience.

4. **Seek Encouragement in Times of Challenge**: When facing challenges, readers can turn to this section for biblical encouragement that speaks to their situation. The verse from Philippians 4:13, "I can do all things

through Christ who strengthens me," under the "Tony Solaita Little League" section, for example, can provide strength and reassurance during difficult times.

5. **Align Principles with Faith**: The Biblical Encouragement section helps readers align their personal growth journey with their faith. As they develop a personal manifesto or a growth plan, they can use these verses to ensure their values and actions are grounded in scriptural truth, much like Habakkuk 2:2's instruction to "Write the vision; make it plain on tablets."

6. **Apply Verses to Everyday Life**: Readers can use the provided verses as reminders to apply the lessons in everyday life. For example, the verse from Galatians 6:9, "Let us not grow weary of doing good," in the "Normalize the Mission" section, can serve as a daily reminder to stay committed to their mission, even when progress seems slow.

Using This Section Effectively:

- **Personal Reflection**: Readers can use the verses to reflect on their own life experiences and how they relate to the themes of each section. This practice encourages introspection and spiritual growth.

- **Goal Setting and Planning**: When setting personal goals or creating a growth plan, readers can draw inspiration from the verses that align with their objectives, ensuring their path is both purposeful and spiritually grounded.

- **Guided Journaling**: Each verse can be a prompt for journaling exercises, where readers explore how the scripture speaks to their current circumstances and what actions they feel called to take.

This section is a resource for readers to connect the dots between faith, culture, and personal development, providing them with a richer and more meaningful reading experience that extends beyond the pages of the book.

1. Introduction

- **Bible Verse**: "For where your treasure is, there your heart will be also." — Matthew 6:21

- **Description**: This verse emphasizes the importance of aligning one's values (treasure) with what truly matters in life. The introduction discusses the idea of being "rooted in culture" and having deep values that guide you through life's challenges. Just as a tree is grounded by its roots, this scripture reinforces the idea of grounding oneself in what is precious and true to the heart.

- **Reference from the Section**: "Like that tree, we too must root ourselves deeply—in our values, in our experiences, and in the cultures that shape us."

2. Hi, I'm Rob Pene

- **Bible Verse**: "I have fought the good fight, I have finished the race, I have kept the faith." — 2 Timothy 4:7

- **Description**: This verse reflects the journey of perseverance and staying true to one's calling, similar to Rob's journey of navigating different environments and staying authentic to himself. It mirrors the idea of continuing to grow and learn despite obstacles.

- **Reference from the Section**: "Growth happens when we lean into discomfort, not away from it."

3. From American Samoa

- **Bible Verse**: "Honor your father and your mother, that your days may be long in the land that the LORD your God is giving you." — Exodus 20:12

- **Description**: This verse resonates with the importance of cultural heritage and honoring one's roots, a key theme in this section. It reflects the value of respecting elders and traditions, which is deeply embedded in the Samoan way of life.

- **Reference from the Section**: "Our culture places a strong emphasis on respect—for elders, for authority, and for the natural environment."

4. Tony Solaita Little League

- **Bible Verse**: "I can do all things through Christ who strengthens me." — Philippians 4:13

- **Description**: This verse speaks to the idea of finding strength and resilience through faith, much like the lessons learned on the baseball field under Tony Solaita's guidance. It connects to the idea that one can face life's curveballs with strength and perseverance.

- **Reference from the Section**: "Life, like baseball, will throw us curve balls. There will be bad hops and unexpected challenges, but with the heart of a warrior, we could handle anything."

5. Importance of Cultural Heritage

- **Bible Verse**: "Remember the days of old; consider the generations long past. Ask your father and he will tell you, your elders, and they will explain to you." — Deuteronomy 32:7

- **Description**: This verse emphasizes the importance of remembering and learning from past generations, a central theme in this section. It aligns with the idea of drawing wisdom and strength from one's cultural roots.

- **Reference from the Section**: "Your cultural heritage is more than just the traditions, customs, beliefs, values, and practices passed down through generations. It is the essence of who you are."

6. Extracting Life Principles

- **Bible Verse**: "Teach me your way, O LORD, that I may walk in your truth; unite my heart to fear your name." — Psalm 86:11

- **Description**: This verse aligns with the idea of seeking guidance to discover one's principles. Just as the psalmist seeks God's truth, this section encourages readers to look inward and define their guiding values.

- **Reference from the Section**: "To extract meaningful life principles, you need to look inward—digging into your experiences, values, and the cultural roots that ground you."

7. Be a Student of Yourself

- **Bible Verse**: "Examine yourselves, to see whether you are in the faith. Test yourselves." — 2 Corinthians 13:5

- **Description**: This verse encourages self-examination and reflection, which is precisely what this section is about—being a lifelong student of yourself to better understand your strengths and areas for growth.

- **Reference from the Section**: "To navigate life's challenges with clarity and purpose, you must become a lifelong student of yourself."

8. Interview Others About You

- **Bible Verse**: "Where there is no guidance, a people falls, but in an abundance of counselors there is safety." — Proverbs 11:14

- **Description**: This verse emphasizes the value of seeking counsel from others, which is exactly what this section encourages—getting feedback to gain insights and grow.

- **Reference from the Section**: "Engaging with those who know you well—family, friends, mentors—can provide valuable insights into how others perceive your strengths, values, and areas for growth."

9. Organize the Data

- **Bible Verse**: "For God is not a God of confusion but of peace." — 1 Corinthians 14:33

- **Description**: This verse reflects the importance of organization and clarity. Just as God brings order, this section emphasizes organizing insights to bring clarity and actionable guidance.

- **Reference from the Section**: "Collecting insights from your self-reflection and interviews is a valuable step in understanding yourself better, but without proper organization, these insights can become overwhelming."

10. Create a Manifesto

- **Bible Verse**: "Write the vision; make it plain on tablets, so he may run who reads it." — Habakkuk 2:2

- **Description**: This verse aligns with the idea of creating a clear and actionable manifesto that guides one's life. It reinforces the importance of writing down your values and principles in a way that is easy to follow.

- **Reference from the Section**: "Your manifesto is a declaration of what you stand for and what you strive to embody in your daily life."

11. Overcoming Setbacks

- **Bible Verse**: "Consider it pure joy, my brothers and sisters, whenever you face trials of many kinds, because you know that the testing of your faith produces perseverance." — James 1:2-3

- **Description**: This verse perfectly encapsulates the idea of overcoming setbacks by viewing them as opportunities for growth and perseverance, which is the core message of this section.

- **Reference from the Section**: "Setbacks are not signs of failure; they are opportunities for growth."

12. Commit to Memory and Practice

- **Bible Verse**: "Do not merely listen to the word, and so deceive yourselves. Do what it says." — James 1:22

- **Description**: This verse speaks to the importance of not just knowing one's principles but living them out daily—committing to practice and making them a natural part of life.

- **Reference from the Section**: "Knowing your principles is important, but to make them a living part of who you are, you must commit them to memory and practice them daily."

13. Building a Support System

- **Bible Verse**: "Two are better than one, because they have a good return for their labor: If either of them falls down, one can help the other up." — Ecclesiastes 4:9-10

- **Description**: This verse highlights the value of having a support system, aligning with the theme of this section that emphasizes surrounding yourself with people who lift you up.

- **Reference from the Section**: "A strong support system is a foundation for growth, resilience, and accountability."

14. Applying Principles in Different Life Contexts

- **Bible Verse**: "Let your light shine before others, so that they may see your good works and give glory to your Father who is in heaven." — Matthew 5:16

- **Description**: This verse encourages applying one's principles consistently in various contexts, much like shining a light in different areas of life to inspire others and live authentically.

- **Reference from the Section**: "Applying principles across different contexts is like a chef using the same ingredients to create a variety of dishes; the core remains the same, but the outcomes are unique."

15. Normalize the Mission

- **Bible Verse**: "And let us not grow weary of doing good, for in due season we will reap, if we do not give up." — Galatians 6:9

- **Description**: This verse underscores the importance of consistency and persistence in one's mission, much like this section emphasizes making daily actions align with your mission.

- **Reference from the Section**: "Make your mission a natural part of your daily routine; consistency is key."

16. Developing a Personal Growth Plan

- **Bible Verse**: "The heart of man plans his way, but the LORD establishes his steps." — Proverbs 16:9

- **Description**: This verse speaks to the importance of planning while trusting that God will guide your path, echoing the idea of developing a flexible yet purposeful growth plan.

- **Reference from the Section**: "The best growth plans are intentional, flexible, and aligned with your values."

17. Revisit and Evolve Your Principles Over Time

- **Bible Verse**: "Do not conform to the pattern of this world, but be transformed by the renewing of your mind." — Romans 12:2

- **Description**: This verse aligns with the concept of continually revisiting and evolving one's principles to stay aligned with one's true self and purpose.

- **Reference from the Section**: "Revisiting your principles keeps them relevant and impactful."

These Bible verses are chosen to complement each section's key message, providing a spiritual anchor that readers can reflect upon as they explore the themes in the book.

Reflective Prayers

The **Reflective Prayers** section is designed to accompany each chapter of "Rooted in Culture," providing readers with a spiritual touchstone to enhance their engagement with the book's themes.

These prayers are crafted to help you internalize the lessons discussed, seek divine guidance, and encourage introspection on your personal growth journey. Each prayer aligns with the specific content of its corresponding chapter, offering a moment of quiet reflection, spiritual grounding, and connection with God.

In a world filled with noise and distractions, these reflective prayers offer a pause—a chance to center yourself, to think deeply about the principles you're exploring, and to connect with the Creator who guides us. They are designed not just as words to be read, but as heartfelt conversations with God that align with your learning and growth.

How to Use This Section Effectively:

1. **Start or End Your Chapter Reading with a Prayer:** Use the reflective prayer for each chapter as a way to set your intentions before you begin reading or as a way to conclude your reflections after finishing a chapter. This helps you to frame your reading within a spiritual context, preparing your heart and mind to receive the lessons with an open spirit.

2. **Integrate the Prayers into Your Daily Devotions:** Consider incorporating these prayers into your daily devotional practice. Reflect on the themes and lessons of each chapter, and then use the corresponding prayer to ask for guidance, strength, and wisdom in applying these lessons to your life.

3. **Journal Your Reflections After Each Prayer:** After reading and praying, take a few moments to journal your thoughts and feelings. How does the prayer resonate with you? What insights or emotions does it bring to the surface? Journaling your reflections can

help solidify the lessons learned and provide a deeper understanding of how God is working in your life through these principles.

4. **Share and Discuss with a Group:** If you are reading this book as part of a study group or with friends, use the prayers as a starting point for group reflection and discussion. Sharing your personal reflections and hearing others' perspectives can provide new insights and strengthen your faith journey together.

5. **Revisit the Prayers Regularly:** Personal growth is a continuous journey, and these prayers are meant to be revisited as you evolve. As you apply the lessons from the book to your life and face new challenges, return to these prayers to seek fresh guidance and reaffirm your commitment to the principles you're developing.

6. **Personalize the Prayers:** Feel free to adapt the prayers to better suit your personal circumstances or needs. Use them as a foundation to build your own prayers that speak directly to your heart and current life situation. Allow the Holy Spirit to guide you in expanding

or modifying these prayers to make them more personal and impactful.

By using the **Reflective Prayers** section thoughtfully and regularly, you can deepen your spiritual journey, enhance your understanding of the book's lessons, and align your personal growth with God's purpose for your life.

Let these prayers be a constant reminder of God's presence, wisdom, and guidance as you walk your path of growth and self-discovery.

Reflective Prayers for each Chapter

Each prayer is designed to complement the themes of the chapters, providing a moment of spiritual reflection that encourages personal growth, deeper understanding, and stronger faith.

Hi, I'm Rob Pene

Reflective Prayer for Self-Awareness and Authenticity

Heavenly Father, I thank You for the unique journey that You have set before me. Help me to embrace who I am, understanding that my story is a testament to Your grace and guidance. May I live authentically, sharing my experiences to inspire others and bring glory to Your name.

From American Samoa

Reflective Prayer for Honoring Roots and Heritage

Lord, I am grateful for the rich cultural heritage You have given me. Help me to honor my roots and the values passed down through generations. May I use my heritage as a source of strength and wisdom, and may it guide me to walk in humility and grace in all that I do.

Tony Solaita Little League

Reflective Prayer for Mentorship and Impact

Gracious God, thank You for the mentors and role models who have shaped me. Help me to be a positive influence in the lives of others, just as they have been for me. May I lead with integrity, teach with patience, and inspire with passion, reflecting Your love in every action.

Importance of Cultural Heritage

Reflective Prayer for Celebrating Diversity and Unity

Heavenly Father, help me to celebrate the beauty and diversity of my cultural heritage while recognizing our unity in You. May I honor my ancestors and the lessons they have passed down, using them to build bridges of understanding and love in a world that so deeply needs both.

Extracting Life Principles

Reflective Prayer for Clarity and Wisdom

Lord, grant me the clarity to discern the life principles that will guide me according to Your will. Help me to be intentional in choosing values that reflect Your truth and love, and give me the courage to live by them every day, no matter the challenges I face.

Be a Student of Yourself

Reflective Prayer for Self-Reflection and Growth

Father, teach me to be a lifelong student of myself, continually seeking growth and deeper understanding. Help me to reflect honestly on my thoughts, actions, and motivations, and to align them with Your purpose for my life. May I grow in wisdom and grace each day.

Interview Others About You

Reflective Prayer for Openness and Humility

Heavenly Father, give me the humility to seek feedback from others and the openness to receive it with grace. Help me to learn from their insights and to see myself through their eyes, that I may grow closer to the person You have called me to be.

Organize the Data

Reflective Prayer for Discernment and Organization

Lord, guide me in organizing my thoughts and experiences in a way that reveals Your truth and wisdom. Help me to see patterns in my life that align with Your will, and to discard those that do not. May I find clarity and direction as I seek to live purposefully.

Craft Your Manifesto

Reflective Prayer for Purpose and Direction

Father, as I craft my personal manifesto, help me to root it deeply in Your Word and in the values that reflect Your love. May this manifesto serve as a guiding light for my life, helping me to stay focused on what truly matters and to live each day with intention.

Overcoming Setbacks

Reflective Prayer for Strength and Resilience

Gracious God, when I face setbacks and challenges, remind me of the strength I have in You. Help me to see obstacles as opportunities for growth and to trust in Your greater plan. May I rise each time I fall, growing stronger in faith and character.

Commit to Memory and Practice

Reflective Prayer for Discipline and Consistency

Lord, help me to commit to the principles that align with Your will and to practice them consistently in my daily life. Give me the discipline to stay focused on my spiritual growth and to embody the values I hold dear, even when it is difficult.

Building a Support System

Reflective Prayer for Community and Support

Heavenly Father, guide me to build a community of like-minded individuals who will support and uplift me on my journey. Help me to be a source of strength and encouragement to others, fostering relationships that reflect Your love and grace.

Applying Principles in Different Life Contexts

Reflective Prayer for Alignment and Integrity

Lord, as I navigate different areas of my life, help me to apply my principles consistently and with integrity. May I be a person of faith in all situations, aligning my actions with my beliefs and standing firm in Your truth.

Normalize the Mission

Reflective Prayer for Consistency and Focus

Father, help me to normalize the mission of living by my principles each day. May I not grow weary in doing good, but rather find strength and joy in the journey. Keep me focused on the path You have set before me, with my heart always anchored in Your love.

Developing a Personal Growth Plan

Reflective Prayer for Guidance and Growth

Gracious God, as I develop my personal growth plan, I seek Your guidance and wisdom. Help me to set goals that honor You and to take steps that lead me closer to the person You have created me to be. May I grow spiritually, emotionally, and mentally under Your care.

Revisit and Evolve Your Principles Over Time

Reflective Prayer for Adaptability and Wisdom

Lord, help me to revisit and evolve my principles as I grow and learn. Give me the wisdom to know when to adapt and when to stand firm, and the courage to follow Your guidance in all things. May I always be open to Your direction and faithful to Your call.

ABOUT THE AUTHOR

Rob Pene, founder of Mission Driven Brand, LLC left the Polynesian islands to pursue his dream of higher education and entrepreneurship. He is a former professional baseball player, spent 6 years as a public school teacher, and has over 15 years of experience in sales and marketing.

When Rob isn't optimizing a website for conversions, he's either hanging out with family, cooking & washing dishes, or on zoom teaching or coaching.

Connect with Rob at his website https://robpene.com

www.ingramcontent.com/pod-product-compliance
Lightning Source LLC
Chambersburg PA
CBHW052348220526
45465CB00003BA/1007